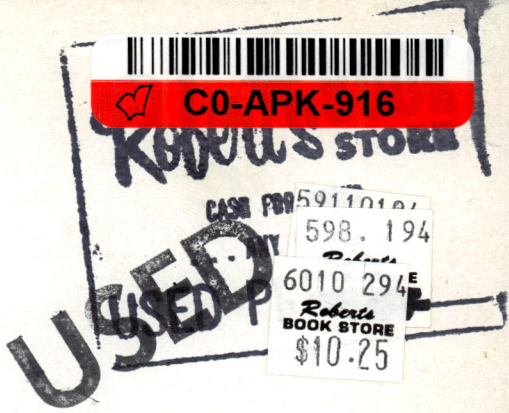

Write in Time

Essay Exam Strategies

Write
In Time
Essay Exam
Strategies

Jeanne F. Campanelli
AMERICAN RIVER COLLEGE

Jonathan L. Price
CALIFORNIA STATE UNIVERSITY, SACRAMENTO

Holt, Rinehart and Winston, Inc.

Fort Worth   Chicago   San Francisco   Philadelphia
Montreal   Toronto   London   Sydney   Tokyo

Publisher: Ted Buchholz
Acquisitions Editor: Michael Rosenberg
Developmental Editor: Stacy Schoolfield
Project Editor: Michael Hinshaw
Production Manager: Tad Gaither
Art & Design Supervisor: Vicki McAlindon Horton
Text Design: Rita Naughton
Cover Design: Candice Swanson

Library of Congress Cataloging-in-Publication Data

Campanelli, Jeanne F.
    Write in time : essay exam strategies / Jeanne F. Campanelli,
Jonathan L. Price.
        p.   cm.
    ISBN 0–03–032593–5
    1. Essay.   2. English language—Rhetoric.   3. Examinations—Study
guides.   4. Study, Method of.   I. Price, Jonathan L.   II. Title.
PE1471.C36   1991
808.4'076—dc20   90–49875
                                                            CIP

Address for Editorial Correspondence
Holt, Rinehart and Winston, Inc., 301 Commerce Street, Suite 3700, Fort Worth,
TX 76102

Address for Orders
Holt, Rinehart and Winston, Inc., 6277 Sea Harbor Drive, Orlando, FL 32887
1-800-782-4479, or 1-800-433-0001 (in Florida)

Printed in the United States of America

1 2 3 4   090   9 8 7 6 5 4 3 2 1

Holt, Rinehart and Winston, Inc.
The Dryden Press
Saunders College Publishing

For my mother and in memory of my father,
Madeline and Lou—JLP

For my mother, Josephine—JFC

Contents

Preface For Students

"Why is a text like this necessary?" "Why must I work on my writing if I am already in college and will enter a profession—such as accounting, engineering, psychology, fine arts or police work—where my writing ability isn't important?" "Why do I need another writing course when I have been receiving passing grades, often A's and B's, on written assignments for other courses?" "What can I expect from this book?" "Will I be able to pass writing exams after using it?"

These are typical, legitimate questions asked by students using this book. Actually, many mature, intelligent individuals—like you—approach the end of a college education (or even complete it) without becoming proficient writers. And yet they will need good writing skills as they enter the careers for which college prepares them.

Initially many students find proficiency exam requirements or books like this one annoying. Students who are not English majors wonder why they should be expected to perform as writers. Yet, if you would think carefully about what professionals do daily, you would see that writing is often required on a regular basis—for reports to outsiders, for explanations to others, for communications with clients who can't be reached by phone. Accountants often must explain in writing, to clients who don't understand numbers, the meaning of those columns of figures, those totals, the interactions of deductions and capital gains; psychologists must often document conditions of clients . . . even artists will often need to give accounts of their work to public agencies, dealers, or art critics to apply for grants or prepare catalogues for shows. All of these require proficiency in writing—solid skills learned now can prove useful later.

Many colleges have instituted a timed-writing exam (or "proficiency exam") as a method of assuring that their graduates have these skills. In such an exam, students are expected to express themselves effectively on a general topic, without preparation and in a limited time. Often colleges create a course to help students prepare for the exam. This text, **Write in Time,** is designed to be used in such a course or to be used by students who need to prepare for a proficiency exam on their own.

We wrote this text for college students and others who need to review writing principles so that they can improve skills in developing and proofreading essays; **Write in Time** is directed toward both freshman and upper division students in order to help them pass a writing proficiency exam. This text will not only help you to pass the exam, it will also help you to write more effectively on in-class written exams for all college classes as well as for other time-limited essay tasks such as entrance exams for postgraduate programs or exams required to certify teachers, accountants or lawyers. In addition, reviewing these principles and profiting from the suggestions offered here should substantially improve *all* your writing, *especially* writing which occurs under time-pressure.

In fact, most writing occurs under some time pressure or other—whether it be an hour for mid-term exams, two hours for finals, one day for writing assignments on a job, one week for essays written as homework, or even three months to a year for a major report, project, or book. In each of these cases, you must divide your writing assignment into various subtasks, allocate your time effectively and be relatively confident of various writing fundamentals ("When do I use a semicolon?" "Where should I begin a paragraph?" "What's the purpose of my final paragraph?") in order to perform proficiently.

Many of you may have earned high grades on papers you've written for classes in your major; but, in many cases, your instructor—as a specialist in another discipline—may have been unwilling to comment on your form, style, or grammar because he or she was concentrating on content. Besides, often such an instructor feels that it is the responsibility of the university as a whole—or the English department—to improve your writing skills. Often, mere lack of practice in composition and lack of *expert* feedback since taking freshman English have caused many students to fall into careless, inadequate, or weak writing patterns.

Many of you may be uncertain, embarrassed, or unhappy with your writing but unwilling to take another composition course. You may think it will be a grueling process or interfere with your other classes, adding even more work to your already overloaded schedule. In fact, the typical student with a high school education and two years of college already has approximately 90 percent of the skills in knowledge, idea development, and awareness of grammar needed to write proficiently. Within a semester, **Write in Time** can help you refine that last 10 percent to make you a proficient, self-assured writer.

But what evidence is there that texts like this work, you might ask? This text was distilled from years of courses designed to help the student achieve proficiency in writing. Courses like these have proven quite effective. For example, for all students taking a junior-level writing exam, the pass rate hovers around 60 percent. Yet for those who fail the first time and merely retake the test, the chance of passing *declines* with each repeat examination, and is as low as 30 percent for those at their *fifth* attempt. On the other hand, recent experience among writing teachers at California State University, Sacramento, shows that students in proficiency courses—all of whom have failed the exam at least once—have an 80- to 90-percent pass rate by the end of the course.

Most students in courses like these also comment that their writing in other classes has improved, and that they now understand (often for the first time), for example, why paragraphs are organized as they are and how to use the semicolon. It is not surprising that education works, but it is rare that we have such clear figures and comments, especially for a product often perceived to be as intangible as writing. Perhaps as you read these words you feel "turned off" to English and writing. However, you now have sufficient education, experience, and maturity to profit from a text which can improve weak writing patterns, overcome misapprehensions about your abilities and make you a confident, proficient writer.

How can you learn to write proficiently? By intelligent practice primarily. Writing is a little like tennis, except that you, the readers of this book, are already intermediate players. But, as in tennis, in order to improve, you need a number of pointers (hints, rules of thumb); then, you must practice those pointers over a period of time. This text consists of pointers for good writing. In order to take full advantage of tennis lessons, you must practice your strokes regularly; in order to take full advantage of this text, you need to practice your writing regularly. A practice essay exam every two weeks—or even more frequently—is effective. A good tennis coach criticizes your style as you practice; a good English professor examines your writing critically. At first, you need your coach or your professor to examine your game or your writing and cirtique it. But eventually, you learn to isolate those qualities which make for a good tennis game or proficient writing and to apply them on your own to your work.

Just as in tennis instruction, you concentrate on one isolated element of the game in each lesson, so in this text, you concentrate on one element of the essay in each chapter. We begin **Write in Time** by examining the qualities of good writing. This will help you to identify critical features in essays of varying quality. Then we show you how to write your own essay: first by pre-writing or idea generation, then by developing the paragraph, and finally by organizing the whole essay from introduction to body to conclusion. We also offer hints for quick proofreading, as well as chapters on improving sentence structure, punctuation, and word choice.

Preface For Instructors

This text is intended as an aid to improving students' writing proficiency. We assume that, as most instructors with composition texts do, you will use it as you see fit, perhaps rearranging chapters, perhaps supplementing it with a handbook—depending on the needs of your students and the teaching strategies you feel comfortable with.

Both in writing the text and in encountering initial reviews, we saw alternative ways to order the chapters. The current order is hardly unassailable, hardly perfect, and certainly not suited to every teaching situation.

Let us explain our rationale for the current chapter order before we suggest some alternative patterns.

We begin with a review of sample exams and scoring levels (Chapter 1) because we want to show students what *passing* exams look like. We also want to show even insecure or failing students that they can easily learn what proficient writing is, and can often intuitively rank exams properly. We believe that even though students who need this text might not *yet* write as well as they would like, they have (as readers, as mature adults) the critical skills to *identify* good writing. A review of sample exams can show such students that they can use those same skills on their own writing.

In the next chapter we offer a series of rules of thumb to help students move quickly from weak to proficient writing. In effect, this chapter is a broad overview of the rest of the text: its rules of thumb are elaborated in the succeeding chapters. The following chapters each address discrete tasks in the writing process—in general, *in the order a writer might perform them during a timed exam:*

3—reading the question, brainstorming, and sketching an approach to the topic

4—using details to develop sound paragraphs

5—forming a clear thesis and using the introductory paragraph as a guide to the entire essay

6—modes of developing body paragraphs, ordering the essay, and constructing transitions

7—concluding paragraphs and quick checking for revision

8, 9, 10, 11—proofreading strategies: typical surface errors, sentences, punctuation, and word choice

We hope that, like us, you don't see the current structure as a straitjacket. Some of you may want to save chapter 1 until the students have finished Chapter 7 (until they know the elements of the essay)—then use 1 (and perhaps 2) to review the overall structure and the elements of proficient writing.

Many of you will notice that Chapters 8, 9, 10, and 11 cover material treated more extensively in handbooks. You may want to skip these chapters because you prefer the handbook (or workbook) approach to surface errors. Or you may skip the material entirely because few of your students display these problems frequently enough to affect their writing proficiency. Whether you use our chapters or a handbook, we suggest that you "sprinkle" parts of these chapters on a regular schedule throughout your course (perhaps once a week in a three-day-a-week course, once every three sessions in a two-day-a-week course) because both instructors and students often find prolonged attention to these issues boring, distracting, or misleading.

Some of you may consider it arbitrary or misleading to include a chapter (4) on developing individual paragraphs before discussing the thesis statement or the essay as a whole (5). We have, however, placed the paragraphing chapter early in the text because we find that the single greatest, recurrent difficulty in weak writers is their lack of detail, their inability to develop generalizations or abstractions. Once they learn how to flesh out a paragraph, to gain confidence in concreteness and detail, many of their other writing problems disappear quickly.

Though we have included a number of exercises, sample exams, and sample proficiency questions, you will probably want to supplement these with questions appropriate to your own state exam, and often with (anonymous) samples of student writing from the class you are currently teaching.

Some of you may feel our standards for proficient writing are too high or too low. We have tried to write a text which will help many students in proficiency classes, not simply to pass, but to exceed the minimum standard for proficiency (in effect, to get a score of 5—see Chapter 1). We have tried as well as to give them sound, practical advice for improving the writing—under all circumstances—they will do in the future.

Acknowledgments

We would like to acknowledge the help of Professors Robert Miles, Charles Moore, Linda Palmer, Floyd McAlister, and Donna Selnick; and the Proficiency Exam staff—especially Beverly Reed—at California State University, Sacramento. We would also like to thank Professor St. George Tucker Arnold III, of Florida International University, for information on the proficiency exam in Florida.

We especially appreciate the confidence and interest in our text shown by the staff at Holt, Rinehart and Winston: our publisher Charlyce Owen, our editors Chris Grooms, Stacy Schoolfield, and Michael Rosenberg, our project editor Michael Hinshaw, and the Northern California representative Sandy Delehanty.

To anyone close to higher education, it is clear that professors don't begin with "perfect knowledge," and that they continue to learn from their students. We acknowledge our great debt to our own students in numerous proficiency exam and other composition classes, especially those in the fall of 1988 and spring of 1989. Particular thanks to Grace Brenneman, Donna M. Davilla, Fawn

Hadley, and Tamara Murphy, whose writing samples—with some alterations—appear in the text.

We want to thank the following reviewers whose comments and advice helped in the development of this text:

Krystan Douglas
University of New Mexico

Michael Prim
Navarro College

Edward White
California State University, San Bernadino

Robert Ratner
Florida International University

Caryl Sills
Monmouth College

Caroline McCarron
College of the Siskyous

Jo Ann Kell
Walter State Community College

Finally, we would like to thank those close to us for their patience and encouragement: Steve Campanelli, Valerie Schmid, David Price, and Gunner Johnson.

Jeanne Campanelli   *Johnathan L. Price*

Write in Time

Essay Exam Strategies

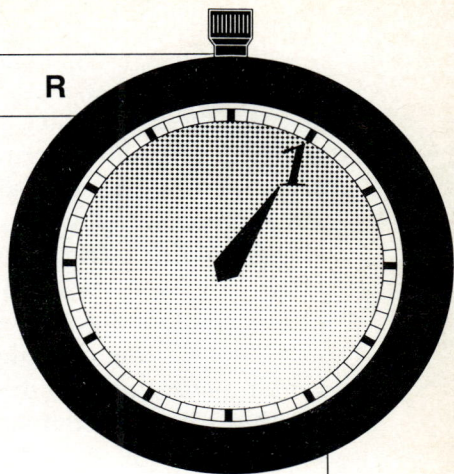

What is Proficient Writing?

SCORING CRITERIA
  Passing Scores
  Failing Scores
4 SAMPLE EXAMS
RANKING THE 4 SAMPLE EXAMS
SAMPLE EXAM CRITIQUES

What is proficient writing? Why is some writing better than other writing? How severely do grammatical and mechanical errors affect proficiency? If a reader can figure out what a writer means, why must writers go through all the trouble of being clear and thorough?

These are important questions student writers ask. They are trying to understand what makes some writing communicate and other writing confuse or annoy readers. Basically, proficient writing is clear, develops ideas with sufficient support, and has few grammatical or mechanical errors. However, determining proficiency in writing is not as simple as counting errors or deciphering a writer's intent in a composition. To understand the concept of proficient writing, we must divide writing into different levels.

Many approaches to writing will involve a ranking system, a method to analyze and compare various writing characteristics. Most writing classes use grades (from A to F, from 0 to 100). Some simply employ a pass or fail; we use a 6-point scale in order to classify writing into groups of relatively equal merit. Scales may vary; however, essentially they classify writing as superior, adequate, inadequate, and very weak.

This system of ranking may at first seem arbitrary to you (most ranking systems are, in some way, subjective), but it will help you to identify characteristics of proficient writing, and ultimately to critically judge your own writing so as to improve it. As in *all* systems of evaluation, whether judging the proficiency of a dive, the value of a painting, or the skill of a gardener, *various* qualities are taken into account and balanced against each other. In effect, this ranking system attempts to be "holistic," to look at the essay as a whole and to judge its elements (such as vocabulary, sentence structure, idea development or organization) as they merge with each other. For example, often an essay that we may consider outstanding in vocabulary is weak in organization—and thus might be ranked equal to an essay that is merely competent in vocabulary use but has a good organization.

SCORING CRITERIA

Here are descriptions of the six levels (Number 6 is the highest):

Passing Scores

6

This is a **superior** paper. It addresses the topic and is noteworthy in both style and content; this paper displays sophistication and creativity. It has a clear, provocative, unifying idea as its thesis. This idea is developed in a variety of ways, in paragraphs that contain solid detail (concrete examples) or sophisticated concepts clearly explained. The essay's organization is clear and easy to follow, with transitions that link thoughts and paragraphs. This careful organization and thorough support indicate a sense of control. Individual sentences are precisely worded and typically reveal a sense of style: sentence structure is varied; vocabulary often reaches above the mundane. There are few, if any, mechanical errors. Frequently this type of essay is creative, original, or unusual in a number of ways.

5

This is a **solid** paper. It addresses the topic, has a clear thesis and a number of paragraphs with more than adequate detail. This paper is carefully organized and transitions establish continuity. The writer is in control of the topic and sure of how to develop it. Individual sentences are precisely worded and present no problems in understanding. Vocabulary is effective, but, compared to a 6, less noteworthy. There may be a few mechanical errors. This essay will be convincing, but not necessarily memorable, striking, or imaginative.

4

This is an **adequate** paper. The writing is competent but not exceptional. It addresses the topic satisfactorily, with a clear thesis and an overall sense of organization, although control over the topic may not be as apparent as in a 5 or 6 paper. Paragraphs are structured and supported with concrete details, but development may be limited or one-sided and transitions may be weak. Sentences are acceptable, but occasional awkward phrasing may cause confusion. Vocabulary is not usually sophisticated, but is properly used. There may be several grammatical and mechanical errors, but these are not a dominant feature of the essay—they are balanced by strengths in the other elements. This essay is clear and readable, but not necessarily creative or memorable. It demonstrates the writing we can expect of an upper division college student composing under time pressure.

Failing Scores

3

Papers at this level are **not proficient**, though they approach proficiency. These papers show an obvious lack of control over the topic. Typically, they are significantly flawed in at least *one* of several ways:

> idea
> organization
> development

word choice, or
mechanics

Perhaps the idea is not clearly stated, or becomes lost as the writer develops the essay—in other words, such an essay may lack focus. Or the organization is poor, and the essay seems to lack planning— paragraphs do not follow each other according to any pattern, or paragraphs seem to stray from the main idea, or perhaps the pattern is purely narrative; often this means that there is much unnecessary or misleading detail. Or the development is weak—often paragraphs lack a topic sentence or lack concrete support and consist primarily of generalizations with little explanation or analysis. Or the word choice and mechanics are highly flawed—most readers would notice and be annoyed or confused by errors such as incorrect word choice, fragments, misspellings, awkward sentences, verb flaws.

2

Papers at this level are **weak**; they do not approach proficiency. They are typically flawed in at least *two* of the following elements: idea, organization, development, word choice, or mechanics. (See comments about these elements under Number 3 above.) Typically, such an essay is weak in paragraph development or organization *and* in mechanics. Weak paragraph development is often demonstrated by consistent use of one- to three-sentence paragraphs. Or the entire essay may be one or two long paragraphs. Lack of planning is apparent—ideas do not flow and frequently seem unrelated. Vocabulary is limited and may be repetitious. Often such essays are difficult to understand because they make only a minor or haphazard attempt to address the essay topic. The writer is unsure and uncomfortable with the task of writing.

1

Papers at this level are rare and make only a minimal attempt at communication. Often they are radically undeveloped, consisting only of one or several short paragraphs; sometimes every other sentence is riddled with awkwardness and mechanical flaws.

In order to understand this 6-point ranking system, let us examine four sample student essays. Read these four essays, first arranging them in descending order of merit, then trying to rank them using the scoring guide.

FOUR SAMPLE EXAMS

Students were given two and a half hours to respond to the following topic:[1]

> The word "education" derives from the Latin for "drawing out." Many people believe that the process of education should involve drawing out or development of students' natural potentials; others, however, note that education often consists of supplying and drilling students with facts, theories, and information designed to be of some practical use after college or in careers.
>
> *Directions:* Write an essay in which you analyze and evaluate your own experiences of American higher education. Indicate what you believe your own natural potential to be; argue as to whether your higher education is drawing it out.

Paper A

Potential in Business Communications

1   When analyzing my experience in American higher education I realize just how much of my own natural potential has been drawn out. I have not only discovered that I can communicate well with others but I have also acquired some understanding of people around me. I have learned to be less judgmental. True it may have taken a few years to come to these conclusions but I feel that it is a direct result of higher education that has opened my eyes to my potential.

2   I can recall when I first decided to become a major in Business Administration. I was attending CSU, Fullerton. I was enrolled in a business class in money and banking. One day the teacher complimented me on my ability to communicate with others. I realized this was true, that I was able to express myself on matters pertaining to business to people at a shared level of understanding.

---

[1]Essay titles have been added for sake of clarity and convenience — students do not usually title their essays in timed exams.

3   Having discovered my potential in business communications has also had an impact on my view of life. Now that I have completed a few courses in my business major I have a better understanding of myself and the people around me. I have learned that this is not just my point of view that matters. It is more beneficial to be objective and have an open mind than it is to be judgmental and closed minded. This I feel creates a better understanding among the associates in business we interact with on a daily basis.

4   In conclusion, because of higher education my potential will continue to grow and I will continue to draw from this experience.

Paper B

From the facts at Solano College to Teaching History in High School

1   Higher education, i.e., college, is designed to broaden one's educational experiences. College is a place where one is able to obtain general as well as explicit knowledge. It has been argued, by some, that the educational process should develop and enhance the natural potential of students. Yet others believe that school is a place where students are given specific information and are expected to reiterate that information, almost word for word, on an exam. While I strongly believe that the school process should attempt to draw out one's natural potential, I will maintain that it is possible for a school of higher education to possess both of these traits.

2   As a first year student at Solano College, I was faced with constant memorization. It seemed as if I was being graded on my ability to remember and repeat exactly what the professor had said on February 7, 1986, in Room 461 of the Science Building, at 1:47 p.m. I was not permitted to interpret the lectures in my own way. I was simply to write down the "facts" as my professor saw them. For instance, the exams required a student to pick one of five multiple choice answers or to mark a response T or F. The professor clearly wanted a specific answer. One was either given full credit or no credit at all. There was no middle ground.

3   Once I began enrolling in classes in my history major, exams drastically changed. Gone were the true/false questions. In their place were essay questions. Now when I take an exam, the professor is looking for my interpretation of the information regardless of how it differs from his or her own opinion. I have experienced both aspects of how higher education is pursued. I believe that the latter is more beneficial to the student because it encourages creative thinking, stimulates the mind, and enhances one's natural potential.

4   As far back as I can remember, I have enjoyed reading history. I have always taken pleasure in reading the lives of heroes such as Lincoln and John F. Kennedy. I also like international relations, and I've particularly enjoyed a course in foreign relations. I feel as if I were born to teach history in high school. I am confident that I can make a difference by making learning a fun experience for all kids. In other words, I believe that it is my natural potential which has enabled me to assist in educating children as I do now, although I am still a student myself.

5   Through attending classes in my field that support individual thought, I feel that my creativity has developed further. Along with the development of my creativity, I feel that I am better able to asses a specific situation and make the best of it. For example, currently I am teaching history to ninth and tenth graders. I was informed of their need for a teacher only a week before the class, and much to my dismay, I wasn't able to locate a copy of their history book. I went into their class without knowledge of what they had covered with the previous teacher. I agonized for hours over what to do with these students for forty-five minutes. Once I was in front of the class, however, the creativity, enhanced through my college courses, took over and I not only managed to teach a lesson on World War II, but I was also able to salvage my peace of mind as well.

6   I am convinced that my natural potential has been encouraged through higher education. If it wasn't for the classes that demanded individual interpretations of historical events, I'd still be reiterating lectures verbatim and answering questions with the letter T or F. I am grateful that certain professors design classes in hopes of enhancing the students' natural potentials, it is truly the best way to learn.

Paper C

Boredom v. Stimulation

1   In the six years I have been attending college (American River and CSUS) most of my classes have seemed much the same. The teachers lectures have been a combination of nothing but facts, figures, and theories. They must think that by learning all these facts, figures, and theories, one would learn that subject they are teaching. Unfortunately, I just get bored with the subject and forget what I have learned after I have taken a test.

2   For my self-esteem, I exspect a lot. Thats why I believe I can do anything I put my mind to. This is what my potential is. The problem with my potential is that it needs to be stimulated. Its very easy for me to get bored and restless, if what I am learning is made up with alot of facts, figures, and theories. Thats why what I learn needs to be interesting and stimulating, for my potential to be drawn out or developed to the fullest possible.

3   When analyzing higher education, I realized that it was not developing or drawing out my fullest potential. The studying of facts, figures, and theories does not help me in learning a subject, it just makes me bored and restless. For the subject to bring out my potential, I need to visualize, experience, and enjoy the subject before I can learn it. I know that is a lot to ask a teacher to teach, but that is why they are teachers. They are there to help bring out or develope one's potential the best way they can, through the subject they teach. Thats why higher education, to me, just seems to be an advanced form of high school where one goes to be bored, and hangs out with their friends.

Paper D *Best*

Creative Writing v. One Person's Ruler

1   "Students, I want you to memorize the correct way to write a composition and I want you to be creative when you write it." With a heavy sigh, I, one of the fortunate students

in the class, felt my head fall to my desk, thinking, "Sure, great, that's what I came to college for . . . to do the impossible!" My professor's instructions were a contradiction in terms; I did not feel I could follow his specific instruction (on word length, paragraph development, minimum number of words per sentence, and so much more) and still have room for creativity. I had an entirely different idea of what creativity was and what my composition should look like. I have experienced many situations such as this one throughout my college education, and now I do not know who to listen to—the soft voice deep inside me or the loud voice of desillusionment I hear when I clash with the established rules and methods. Deep within me I believe I could be a short story writer, but my experiences with American higher education have only served to discourage me from pursuing any natural potential I might have. My desillusionment began with a particular teacher I had in English, continued through my French major and ultimately climaxed in a short story writing class.

{ Thesis statement

} transition

2   My first classroom clash occurred my freshperson year. I took English 1A my first semester and found it thoroughly exhilarating. The professor gave many examples of creative writing styles, encouraged "attention-getters" (in the first paragraph), and accepted varying styles and techniques in writing. Her tolerance and encouragement prompted me to continue the following semester with English 1B. The writing requirements of this teacher represented an entirely different world. This second professor expected every student to conform to a specific set of "proper" rules in writing a "proper" composition.

3   The nightmare began when she listed her numerous criteria and told us that exceptions would be "down-graded" and receive a lower grade. Her list included such criteria as: a "good" sentence should have between 20-27 words in it, a "good" paper should have one or no more than two paragraph margins per sheet of paper (typed), compositions using the verb "is" more than three times will be "down-graded," the thesis should always be at the end of the first/introductory paragraph, and many, so many more requirements which do not necessarily constitute a "good" paper which will be interesting, refreshing, or informative. The class depended too heavily on one person's view of what

creativity should look like. I wanted a class that would encourage me, draw out my potential, and give me room to grow. I suffered through the semester and decided, "No, I don't want to have an English minor when my own judgment or sense of creativity are not involved in the total picture!" That's when I turned to a different language.

4   The French language and major seemed so different and romantic that I thought this would be the haven I was searching for. I am a native speaker so didn't need the monotonous, or so I hear, lower division courses. I enrolled in various grammar courses which would give me the skills I needed to begin to write. One course stands apart in my memory, French Literature 100, Introduction to Fiction. There we covered how to examine short stories and look for such things as theme, setting, character development, symbolism, etc. Like my English 1A experience, it was exhilarating! I enjoyed it thoroughly and wanted to write like many of the authors we discussed. I continued taking literature courses, which I still enjoy, but the composition courses are still the same disheartening experience — one person's ruler used to measure the student's worth (or in this case, writing potential). Ironically enough, my literature courses encourage my writing more than my writing courses. I think the ideal would be a course in which we briefly examine writing styles (from specific authors) and then try to experiment with or apply that writing manner. This combination of styles and experimentation would allow the student to grow and possibly develop his/her own potential. Nonetheless, I'm still at CSUS and struggling with my writing and creative writing classes.

5   The short story course was the creative writing class which has most destroyed my belief in my own potential. Writing is a personal experience for me. I have been trying to write short stories since adolescence and have enjoyed it very much until it became a scheduled thing. The instructor had very good intentions and good ideas which helped me, but he also did two things which discouraged me greatly. He had us share every one of our stories with the class, which lessened my desire to write, and he had a long list of scheduled stories to be written, which shut off all my creative juices. Sharing my inner thoughts and emotions with 20 strangers intimidated me, but scheduling my inspiration

made me lose total interest for years after this class. Fortunately, I have rekindled my interest in the short story.

6   This clash of method and theory against creativity has been a major problem throughout my years of higher education. I have fought against it unsuccessfully. I find this method and approach very unnatural for my writing and detrimental to my potential as a writer.

RANKING THE FOUR SAMPLE EXAMS

Most trained readers would rank these four essays in the following descending order of proficiency:

Paper D   "Creative Writing v. One Person's Ruler"

Paper B   "From the facts at Solano College to Teaching History in High School"

Paper A   "Potential in Business Communications"

Paper C   "Boredom v. Stimulation"

SAMPLE EXAM CRITIQUES

Now let us isolate and examine those elements which characterize these essays and link them to the criteria on our 6-point scale:

Paper D would receive a 5; it is a good example of a solid essay: clear organization, good use of detail, effective vocabulary, few grammatical or mechanical errors. (In fact, because of the writer's imaginative use of quotations and thorough explanations, some graders might give this essay a 6.) It begins with an interesting introduction that ends by stating the thesis, or main focus, of the essay in the final two sentences of paragraph 1. The second of these two sentences unifies the essay by providing a road map to the writer's experience of education—from a particular teacher in her English 1A to a disappointing climax in her short story writing class. This makes the essay's organization clear and easy to follow: we know why the writer proceeds from English composition to a major in French literature to a creative writing class. Thus, the order of paragraphs in the body of the essay makes sense in terms of its thesis. Throughout the essay, the writer focuses on her thesis—that attending college has discouraged her from developing her natural potential—and she provides thorough, clear and relevant support. She also establishes continuity by providing transitions within and between paragraphs. This writer is clearly in control of her topic and knows precisely what she wants to say.

Each paragraph is well developed with concrete examples. In paragraph 2, for instance, the writer identifies a class in which the professor taught "facts," "theories," and a "specific set of proper rules." Then she helps us as readers to understand what writing under those rules was like by specifying some of them: 20-27 words per sentence, no more than two paragraphs per page, only three uses of the verb "is," and so on. In addition, she analyzes the effects of her experience; and her view that this technique was "disillusioning" is clearly explained—she points out that rules like this do not necessarily lead to refreshing or interesting writing, that they do not encourage a student's creativity.

Moreover, sentences are carefully constructed and easy to read, and the writer is adept at varying her sentence structure. For example, though she is discussing herself and classes she took, most sentences do not begin with "I" or "this class." Also, she varies her punctuation skillfully; for example, in paragraph 1 she uses both the semicolon and the dash correctly and effectively.

The writer's diction, or word choice and arrangement, is impressive. For example, she makes effective use of direct quotation at the beginning of the first paragraph and the end of the third paragraph. The teacher's quoted opening speech gives the reader an excellent sense of that classroom atmosphere as well as the double-bind in which the teacher's philosophy of composition put this student. The second quotation captures the student's stream-of-consciousness dilemma about her educational future. Phrases such as "one person's ruler" are imaginative analogies that reinforce the writer's disillusionment with arbitrary rules and education that drills students with facts. This writer also has a polished vocabulary; she is comfortable using common words but able to produce variety and specificity in her writing, with such words as "disillusionment," "exhilarating," "nightmare," "disheartening," and "rekindled."

There are no grammatical errors, but even superior essays written under pressure may have a few mechanical flaws: this writer misspelled <u>disillusionment</u>.

Paper B would receive a 4. This essay begins with an adequate introduction, though this writer's approach lacks the flair and creativity found in Paper D. The thesis in Paper B (final sentence of the introduction) addresses the topic and suggests that education is *both* a "rote" and a "drawing out" process. But this thesis is relatively vague and does not provide a very useful road map to what the essay contains. In fact, the writer's development is not as balanced as his thesis suggests; though he does write a paragraph on the "rote" process, the rest of the essay emphasizes his preference for a "drawing out" process he experienced in his history classes.

Though the essay is organized and moves from a class that emphasizes facts at Solano College to the history classes that emphasize drawing out the student's potential, the organization is not entirely successful or clear, and it lacks transitions. There seems to be an abrupt progression in paragraph 4, where the focus moves from historical heroes to international relations, to an interest in educating children. This paragraph also seems out of place in the writer's overall sequence and perhaps could have been incorporated into the introduction. Had the writer provided better transitions between his ideas, he might have worked out these problems.

Most paragraphs are sufficiently developed, with concrete detail and analysis. For example, notice how the writer uses absurdly specific details in paragraph 2—1:47 p.m., Room 461—to suggest a rote learning process. Still, by comparison, we can see that the writer of Paper D is willing to expand ideas more fully and provide a greater wealth of *relevant* detail than the writer of Paper B, who sometimes strays from his point with too many insignificant details. For example, in paragraph 5 of Paper B, the writer concentrates too much on the details of his agonizing situation and not enough on how his education helped him solve his problem.

Sentence control is sufficient; sentences are readable, and though a number (particularly in paragraph 4) begin with a repetitive structure (I can remember, I have enjoyed, I have taken pleasure, I like, I feel, I am confident), none are difficult to understand or to read. However, "a fun experience" is colloquial phrasing that appears awkward in the more formal structure of a written exam (since "fun" is usually used in writing as a noun, not an adjective). Overall, this writer's vocabulary is appropriate, but lacks the interesting variety found in Paper D.

There are few mechanical flaws, but the writer does misspell assess and joins two independent clauses with a comma in the final sentence. This is a "comma splice"; the comma should be replaced with a semicolon or period (see Chapter 10 for a detailed discussion of commas).

Paper A should receive a 3; it is not proficient. Though it has a clear thesis (that college has drawn out his ability to communicate) and the writer attempts to organize ideas in the introduction, the essay is simply undeveloped. Though the writer repeats in each paragraph that his education has helped him develop his ability to communicate, he fails to offer any detail. For example, in paragraph 2 he mentions a "class in money and banking" in which a teacher complimented him on his ability to communicate with others, but he gives no particulars on the circumstances: who he communicated with or what he communicated about. Was he giving a speech? Leading a class discussion? Tutoring other students? He also fails to give an example of a particular occasion when he learned to accept another's point of view—or what that point of view was. In effect, this essay is a series of broad generalizations verging on cliches: "communicate well," "some understanding of people around me," "less judgmental," "better understanding of myself," "beneficial to be objective," "have an open mind." Backing up these generalizations with more specific examples and explanations would aid the reader. Lack of development skill is also shown in the writer's abrupt, one-sentence conclusion; beginning the conclusion with "in conclusion" is mechanical and tedious.

Sentences and mechanics are marginally acceptable, but contain a number of flaws. The writer could improve sentence fluency by using commas to separate independent clauses linked with "but": "I have not only discovered that I can communicate well with others⊙ but I have also acquired some understanding of people around me." The writer could also improve sentence variety; for example, in paragraph 2, four of the five sentences begin with the word "I."

Paper C should receive a 2. It is weak in several ways: idea, development, and mechanics. The writer makes no attempt to write an introduction; further, the opening paragraph contains no thesis or main idea unifying the essay—it simply states that facts and theories bore him. Nor does the writer attempt to organize the essay; he seems to be writing randomly, putting down whatever happens to come to mind. Without a clear thesis and a sense of organization, the writer is unable to develop his essay in unified paragraphs—so there is only one paragraph of "development," and that is only about potential. But the writer never identifies any particular potential, never refers to a particular class, discipline, idea, day, or week. Instead, he implies or hints at problems in the education system, expecting the reader to understand and agree with him. This writer needs to anchor his ideas with concrete examples, which would give him a way of developing a variety of body paragraphs. The writer's third paragraph, or conclusion, does little more than repeat what he said in his first two paragraphs.

Even in so short an essay, there are numerous patterns of mechanical and grammatical flaws: the writer often omits necessary apostrophes (teachers⊘ lectures, that⊘s why, It⊘s very easy). The writer misspells <u>expect</u> and <u>develop</u> and misplaces "were" for <u>where</u>. Further, paragraph 3 (sentence 3) contains a comma splice, and the pronoun "their" in the final sentence refers to "one," a confusion of singular and plural. Inappropriate tense shifts are another grammatical flaw; for example, in paragraph 3 the writer shifts from present ("when analyzing") to past ("I realized") to present ("the studying . . . does not help me"). The writer's tendency to repeat ("facts, figures and theories") becomes annoying and suggests a limited vocabulary.

EXERCISE 1-1

Read the question posed below and examine the two essays following according to the 6-point ranking scale. Rank each essay with a number and identify criteria which caused you to assign that rank. (Students completed the following essays in 1 hour and 15 minutes.)

THE ISSUE: A law in some states requires high school students to maintain a grade of at least C- in every class in order to be eligible to participate in extracurricular activities. The law attempts to assure that outside activities not interfere with students' main purpose in school: to learn academic subjects. However, some feel it is unfair to exclude a student entirely from extracurricular activities even if the student should drop below a C- in a class. These critics argue that students who excel in sports, for example, should not be penalized because they are weak in English.

THE TOPIC TO WRITE ON: Drawing from your personal experience, knowledge and observations, argue as to whether the "C-Minus Law" is a fair requirement for high school students.

A.

C- Rule Removes Athletes from Pedestals

1   How many professional athletes in this country are illiterate due to their high school teachers sliding them through classes in order for them to make football or

basketball practice? How many high school "jocks" have never opened a text book because their coach expected them to run that extra 5 miles? The illiteracy rate in this country alone is staggering; something needs to be done! I feel the California law requiring high school students to maintain a grade of at least C- in order to participate in extracurricular activities is a step in the right direction. The "C Minus Law" is a fair requirement because it does not allow favoritism among students, or make the high school jock out to be bigger than life.

2   Teachers showing unnecessary favoritism towards students who participate in extracurricular activities (especially sports) occurs in high school classes all across the nation. I can remember my Federal Government teacher in high school letting the football players in the class off easy compared to what was required from the rest of the class. For example, when it came to homework and tests, the football players were always given an additional week to makeup the assignment, or the assignment was overlooked completely. This behavior made it to easy for these players to receive even a C-. In addition, if these players needed to attend an early practice or game, they were always dismissed early. I believe this favoritism was unjust in that it placed football (sports) above academic achievement. These football players were being allowed to slide by with the minimum of work missing out on learning and improving their academic skills. Therefore, the "C- law" is definitely needed to keep athletes in the classroom.

3   Moreover, our society places to much emphasis on professional athletes. Similarly, high school campus's place their exceptional athletes on pedestals. But, are these athletes knowledgeable in literature and educated in the basics of reading, writing and arithmetic? I have seen and heard professional athletes interviewed on television who could barely put together a coherent sentence. This alone shows society needs to start placing more emphasis on the 3 R's starting in high school, and less on promoting extracurricular activities; this is where the C- law comes into effect. Finally, America is waking up and realizing that students need to be well educated before they can take up that extracurricular activity. The "C- law" is a step in the right direction because it encourages students to read and excel in the classroom before they hit the field.

4   The "C- law" is an effective tool because it will slowly but surely make our countries illiteracy rate drop. Our country does need athletes, but it needs athletes who are also educated. I also believe we should stop placing so much emphasis on high school extracurricular activities, and more on the 3 R's.

B.

C- Rule Unfair to High School Athletes

1   The roar of the crowd is deafening. Number eighty-nine has just scored the winning touchdown for his high school team. He is being courted by every major college in the nation, yet he won't be allowed to play in next weeks game. By not playing in his team's next contest number eighty-nine will lose his chance at a college scholarship. Simply because number eighty-nine is receiving a "D" in chemistry. A state law requires high school students to maintain a C-grade or better in every class. This "C minus law" is totally unfair to today's youth. The "C minus" law could potentially prevent gifted athletes from receiving college scholarships, it gives them no second chance. I had a good friend academically disqualified during my senior football season.

2   During my junior year in high school there was a star player named Jack Abrams on a rival team. Jack was the whole team, during his game against us he caught ten passes and ran for one-hundred and fifty yards. Jack had every major college in the western United States trying to recruit him. But, it seemed Jack wasn't very proficient at Geometry. He received a D midway through his final high school season. Jack was disqualified after the third game of his senior season. It seems that all the major colleges forgot about Jack, and being from a poor family he ended up doing landscaping with his father. A similar situation occurred in Wheaton just two years ago.

3   Marc Bagley was the standout running back for Wheaton High. He too was recruited by nearly every major college in the United States. During Marc's senior season, Marc set state records for most yards rushing in a game, most yards rushing in a season, and most touchdowns scored in a game. Marc was, and is, a truly gifted athlete, yet

his overall grade point average was barely above a C. Marc managed to receive nothing below a C on his midseason report card and was able to finish Wheaton highs football schedule. Today Marc is the starting tailback for Notre Dame and is scheduled to graduate next year. What if Marc had dropped below a C and was disqualified? Where would he be today, mowing lawns? Instead Marc will graduate from one of the most prestigious colleges in the nation, and possibly have a shot at the National Football League. While I never had a chance to make the N.F.L., I did play high school football.

4   My senior year in football was a dream come true. My team won our section for the third straight year and I was named all-league. Unfortunately my good friend Dave wasn't so lucky. Dave has a three point eight grade point average going into our senior year. Dave wasn't planning on playing college ball, but he was an excellent high school center. Regrettably Dave was unaware of the "C minus" law. Since he had such great grades in the past Dave figured he didn't have to apply himself during the football season. Dave received a D in creative writing midway through the season and was academically disqualified. While the rest of the team and I won the section championships, Dave watched from the stands. To this day Dave expresses remorse over missing his last season.

5   All of these are examples of how the "C minus" law can backfire. Jack, Marc, and Dave were adversely affected by this unfair law. It seems that good athletes and good students are penalized alike. Lets hope there will be no more Jacks in the world.

SUMMARY

1. A proficient essay is clear, organized, and develops its idea in sufficient detail, using variety in sentence structure and word choice; also, it displays few errors in grammar or mechanics.
2. Proficient essays interest and inform readers; they do not confuse readers with vague or irrelevant information.
3. Nonproficient essays fail in one or more ways—they may be weak because they are vague or imprecise or misleading or self-contradictory; they may not develop an idea in sufficient

detail; they may display a number of grammatical or mechanical errors.

4. Learning how to score others' essays holistically is the beginning of skillfully evaluating your own writing and becoming a proficient writer.

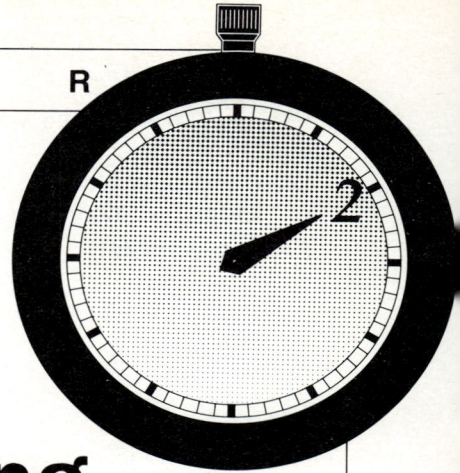

Taking A Timed Writing Exam: Rules of Thumb

PLANNING
  Time Limits—A Fact of Life
BRAINSTORMING
  Directive Words/Key Words
DRAFTING AND CHECKING
  Introduction
  Unifying Ideas For Paragraphs
  Conclusion and Checking
PROOFREADING

You have been given an exam question and have a limited time in which to respond. As the clock ticks away, you read and re-read the question. Your mind may be blank, or it may be filled with so much to say you don't know where to start. You know you must be organized and thorough; but you're not sure of just where to begin, how much to say, and when to conclude. This chapter will show you some important strategies to use in taking a writing proficiency examination or any timed writing exam. These "rules of thumb" will help you to quickly formulate an approach to writing and to organize and develop your ideas within your time limit.

Rules of Thumb

1. Have a plan for writing.
2. Allow time for brainstorming to generate and organize your ideas.
3. Identify the directive and key words in your exam question and use them to focus your brainstorming and formulate your essay.
4. Begin writing immediately.
5. Construct an outline from your brainstorming notes to guide you in writing your first draft.
6. Write an introductory paragraph that states your thesis and sets up body paragraphs.
7. Make sure each body paragraph has a unifying idea.
8. Avoid writing one-sentence or one-page paragraphs.
9. Write a conclusion and check your essay for content and structure.
10. Allow time to proofread your draft carefully for errors in grammar and mechanics.

PLANNING

Rule of Thumb #1: Have a plan for writing. Most activities require planning if they are to turn out successfully. A camping trip, for example, begins with gathering and checking all the camping equipment, shopping for food, selecting a campground or camping spot, obtaining a burning permit if necessary, and loading the car. You perform each step of the plan in a certain order, and often you may write lists to remind yourself of what you need: a list of equipment, a list of food, a list of possible camping sites. If you fail to plan your trip carefully, you might find yourself out in the wilderness without sleeping bags, or propane fuel for your lantern, or matches to light the campfire! Work-related activities also require careful planning—often according to a time schedule to meet a deadline. In a restaurant, for example, certain "opening" tasks, such as setting tables, lighting candles, refilling salt and pepper shakers, and chilling wines, must be completed before the customers arrive. Likewise, a teacher must plan lessons for each day's class;

a construction foreman must schedule his crew's workload; an accountant must gather information and complete her client's tax forms by April 15. At work or play, people don't usually jump into tasks haphazardly—they follow a plan. Writing—especially on a proficiency exam—is no different.

In previous classes you may have experienced the planning process involved in writing. For a research paper, for example, your instructor may have required you to turn in a bibliography and note cards to get your research started, an outline to get your information organized, and a rough draft to flesh out your ideas—all due at intervals, before your final paper. In an English class, an instructor may have required you to submit an outline, then a draft, before you turned in your essay (in addition, you may have had to revise what you thought was a final draft). The difference between these writing situations and a proficiency exam is the amount of *time*—but not the need for *planning*. Whether you have all semester or just two hours in which to write about a subject, you should follow a writing plan. You should make this plan ahead of time, so that when you actually take your exam you will already have a strategy to get you going and will not waste time wondering where to begin. In fact, the shorter the time limit, the more critical it is to have a plan. When your time is restricted, you cannot afford to waste one minute. A writing plan gives you direction—a method with which to approach your essay. Your plan should include **brainstorming and organizing your ideas, drafting and checking,** and **proofreading** your final draft for accuracy. Your plan must also restrict the amount of time you spend on each of these tasks so that you can finish your essay within your time limit.

The Three Stages of Writing

1. BRAINSTORMING AND ORGANIZING IDEAS
2. DRAFTING AND CHECKING
3. PROOFREADING

TIME LIMITS—A FACT OF LIFE

"If I only had one more hour—I could have aced that exam!" "I was writing until the proctor grabbed my paper out from under my pen." "No matter how much time they give you, it's never enough. . . ." Students frequently complain, when they must take an essay examination, that they do not have enough time to organize **and** express all their ideas **and** edit **and** proofread their essays. Students claim that they can perform much better when they have a day or two to sort out their ideas, write several rough drafts, think, read and reread, and correct mistakes. And these students are right!

Racing against the clock to finish causes pressure and often prevents students from performing proficiently. However, a time limit is inevitable for any examination: GRE, LSAT, writing proficiency and so forth. Moreover, *all* writing is done under some kind of time limit: a journalist must have the story done in time for the next day's paper; a manager must have the report written before the next week's board meeting; a student has perhaps a month in which to complete a research paper. Even this text—which was not required writing for the authors—was written according to deadlines. Writers, student and professional alike, may think they don't want to be encumbered by a deadline, but without one, they may never see their finished products.

When your time is extremely limited, as is the case for essay exams, a time/task plan will alleviate some of the pressure and enable you to perform proficiently. The plan suggested here is *flexible;* you may combine some tasks and allot more or less time depending upon your personal writing habits. The point is that a proficient essay is written in consecutive stages; you must make time for each stage in your writing plan.

> Stage 1—**Brainstorming and arranging ideas**—allot about one-fifth of your time
>
> Stage 2—**Drafting and Checking**—allot about three-fifths of your time
>
> Stage 3—**Proofreading**—allot about one-fifth of your time

BRAINSTORMING

Rule of Thumb #2: Allow time for brainstorming to generate and organize your ideas. The first task in your writing plan is brainstorming: **analyzing your topic, generating information for your essay and organizing that information into some kind of structure.** (Brainstorming and organizing techniques are discussed in more detail in Chapter 3.) On a two-hour essay exam, for example, you should allot approximately 10-25 minutes, or no more than one-fifth of your total time, **for deciding what you want to say**

and in what order you want to say it. You should think of brainstorming as a kind of warm-up period. Just as a runner stretches his muscles before a race, writers should take time to explore what they have to say—or "stretch their minds"—about an exam subject through brainstorming. Once you see your thoughts on paper, you can more easily decide which ones are worth pursuing and which may not work. By narrowing your focus and eliminating ineffective ideas in the brainstorming stage, you will avoid wasting time writing on unproductive ideas in your draft stage.

Directive Words/Key Words

Rule of Thumb #3: Identify the Directive and Key Words in your exam question and use them to focus your brainstorming and formulate your essay. Proficient writers are able to correctly interpret the topic on which they must write and respond appropriately. Most writing proficiency exams require you to write spontaneously on a question you have never seen before, though you are probably familiar with the subject matter in some way. Usually proficiency exam questions ask you to draw from your knowledge and personal experience and discuss issues such as women's liberation, the benefits and drawbacks of modern technology, the value of a college education, or the impact of a leader. These typical subjects are not difficult; you have probably thought about, discussed, or even written about them before. But what exactly should you say in your essay? How much should you write? What approach should you take?

The answers to these questions really lie in your **exam question**. When you buy something that requires assembly—a new camping tent, for example—you rely on the directions that come with the tent to fit all the parts together properly. If you don't read the directions at all, or read them only superficially, you may omit important steps and end up with a haphazard finished product: your tent won't stand up; one side is higher than the other; the center pole is too short. Had you read and followed the directions carefully, you would not be racing against the sunset to pitch your tent! Most exam questions are like instructions or directions; if you read them carefully, you'll find particulars as to what you should write about, how you should develop your ideas, even how many paragraphs you should write. Your exam question may also give you specific information as to how all your "parts"—or ideas—fit together to form a proficient essay. Finally, your question will help you establish your writing plan—so you won't be racing against the clock to finish your exam.

Therefore, you must look for **directive words**, or "command words" as they are sometimes called, in the exam question which will help you to respond appropriately. Not only will these words help you to understand what to write about, but they will also help you to formulate paragraphs, so you will get a feel for how long your essay should be. Let's first take a look at some common directive words; then we will examine how these words function in typical exam questions and how you can use them in the brainstorming process.

Directive Words

Analyze—break into parts to discover relations between the parts; determine *why* events occurred as they did or *why* you feel as you do about an issue; discuss causes and effects; explain your opinions or interpretations; reveal facts and truths. Similar directive words include **evaluate, examine, explain.**

Argue or support—take a stand for or against an issue and give evidence and reasons why you believe as you do. Similar directive words include **justify** and **defend.**

Describe—depict or portray; recreate with *carefully selected* details so the reader can understand. This term can also involve **narrating** an event (in story form) so the reader can understand what happened. Similar directive words include **relate** and **tell about**.

Discuss—talk about a subject from *more than one perspective*; point out several aspects; investigate or contemplate *several* important points. Sometimes your discussion will focus on a **comparison** or a **contrast**.

(Note: **describe** and **narrate** are the only directives that do not require personal judgments.)

Once you identify the directive words in your exam question you can use them to start the brainstorming process. Circle the directive words, then write them down on scratch paper. Also write down other **key words** that suggest specific ideas as you read your topic. Key words are words that suggest *specific ideas* related to your directive words: analyze *an inefficient procedure*, discuss *the qualities of a good leader*, describe *a situation that led you to a compromise*. These directives and key words will help you organize your essay and generate pertinent information. Some exam questions have **sequential** directive words; for example, you may be asked to **describe** a situation, then **discuss** it, then **analyze** why it happened as it did **in that specific sequence**. Other questions are more open-ended and use only one or two directive words, leaving the writer more freedom to determine sequence. In either case, directive words will help you frame your essay structure. Now let's examine how directive words are used in writing proficiency exam topics and how they can help you approach your essay.

> *Question #1*—The process of growing older has both positive and negative aspects. DISCUSS some of these aspects and EXPLAIN why you believe aging is ultimately a positive or a negative experience.

In this topic, the directive words **DISCUSS** and **EXPLAIN** give you a general idea of what you must cover in your essay; but you also want to look for key words that will give you specific ideas—a perspective for your directive words. For example, the words "positive," "negative," and "aging" give you a particular focus as to what to DISCUSS and EXPLAIN. You will use these words to start brainstorming, to generate details for your essay (Chapter 3 discusses methods to generate information).

The first directive word, **DISCUSS**, indicates that you need to examine the issue of aging from **more than one perspective**; in this case, you can focus on both positive and negative aspects, as your question further suggests. Thus, your discussion will be a kind of comparison/contrast. You will probably want to select two or three positive aspects and two or three negative aspects of aging and devote *one paragraph to positive aspects* and *one paragraph to negative*.

For example, your positive paragraph could begin with the following topic sentence, or statement of the unifying idea[1]:

---

[1]A **topic sentence** is a statement, usually one sentence, of the *main idea* you are going to write about in a paragraph. This is the idea that all the details in the paragraph will support. You may have heard or read other terms used to refer to the topic sentence: main idea, controlling sentence, governing statement, commitment statement. In this text, we have chosen the term *unifying idea* to refer to the topic sentence in a paragraph because the term "unifying" suggests that this statement *unifies*, or *brings together*, all the support sentences in a paragraph.

"Gaining wisdom through experience and developing a greater understanding of others are two positive aspects of the aging process." You could then discuss how a person benefits from life experiences and how a person grows to understand human nature as he or she gets older. (If you thought your paragraph was getting too long, you might decide to cover *life experiences* and *understanding human nature* in two separate paragraphs.) Your negative paragraph could begin with this unifying idea: "While the rewards of aging are mental, the negative aspects of aging are primarily physical: a person's appearance and health deteriorate as he grows older." Your discussion in this paragraph would focus on how aging affects physical beauty and causes health problems. (Again, if your negative paragraph seemed too long, you could discuss, for example, the deterioration of appearance in one paragraph, and illness in another paragraph.)

Then in a third paragraph, you could take a stand—decide if you feel aging is either beneficial or detrimental and carefully **EXPLAIN**, or rationalize why you feel as you do. For example, let's say you feel the wisdom and understanding gained as a person gets older are far more important than good looks or perfect health. You will clearly state your point of view and the reasons why you hold that view in a unifying idea at the beginning of this paragraph. Again, limit your reasons, so you can cover them thoroughly in the paragraph. Add an introduction and a conclusion to this essay and you have covered the subject in five to seven paragraphs.

The approach to the aging question was straightforward; just by following the directive and key word clues, you could develop the essay. Other questions, however, may be more complex; there may be more than one approach to developing an essay. For example, consider the following question:

> *Question #2*— Most people feel that the experience of attending college changes them in either obvious or subtle ways. Drawing from your personal experience and observations, ANALYZE ways in which the experience of attending college causes people to change. DISCUSS the drawbacks and/or benefits of the changes.

In this question, the directive words **ANALYZE** and **DISCUSS** give you a general idea of how to approach this topic; the more specific key words **college, changes, drawbacks** and **benefits** tell you what you should analyze and discuss. So before you even begin writing, you have a clear idea of what to write about (college changes, benefits and drawbacks) and how to write about it (discuss and analyze). This question could be handled in one of two ways.

One approach is to write one paragraph in which you **ANALYZE** the changes college brings about in people (limiting the number of changes to two or three so you can cover them thoroughly in the paragraph), followed by a paragraph in which you **DISCUSS** the benefits or drawbacks of *each* change. For example, your first paragraph could begin with a unifying idea that states the changes: "The experience of attending college helps a student set goals, manage time more effectively, and become more self-confident." In your second body paragraph, you could examine if the changes were good and why. A unifying idea for this paragraph could be: "The changes college brings about enable a student to handle the real world demands of job and family." With an introduction and a conclusion, this essay would have *four* fairly long paragraphs.

Another approach, however, is to **ANALYZE** each change *in a separate paragraph*, discussing the benefits or drawbacks *as you analyze the change*. The number of paragraphs in this essay would be determined by the number of changes you discuss. For example, if your introduction indicated that attending college gives students more direction in life, increases students' self-confidence and forces them to be more organized, you would follow with *three body paragraphs*: one on gaining direction, one on increased self confidence, and one on becoming more organized. In each paragraph, you would not only explain the change, but also you would discuss the benefits or drawbacks of the change. In a paragraph on learning to be more organized, for instance, you might point out that, although being organized helps a student to accomplish a variety of activities efficiently, a structured life leaves little room for spontaneous ventures. Add a conclusion to this essay and you have written five paragraphs.

The questions on aging and on the changes brought about by college are typical of the more open-ended proficiency questions; both have only two directive words, yet by combining directives with key words, a writer can adequately develop an essay for either question. Open-ended questions allow writers leeway in deciding how many paragraphs to include in the essay and what order the paragraphs will follow. Multiple directive questions, or questions with three or more directive words in a specific sequence, are somewhat different.

While the multiple-directive question gives the writer a specific idea of how many paragraphs to write (usually one paragraph per directive word), what each paragraph should be about and the sequence of the paragraphs, writers must respond to this type of question more precisely. If writers omit a part of the multiple directive question, or change the directive sequence, their essays may turn out underdeveloped or unorganized. Here is a typical multiple-directive question (directive words are capitalized).

> DESCRIBE a situation when you felt the need to be alone, and EXPLAIN your reasons for wanting to be by yourself. DISCUSS the reaction of your family and friends to your need to be alone, and ANALYZE what you learned from their reaction to your desire for solitude. Finally, EVALUATE what you learned about yourself from your experience of being alone.

The five directive words in this question—**describe, explain, discuss, analyze** and **evaluate**—suggest that the essay might have at least five paragraphs. (You could possibly combine the first two directives in one long paragraph; but if the situation when you needed to be alone was quite detailed, you should describe it in a separate paragraph to avoid confusion.) Also, if you approached the question in any other sequence besides the order in which the directives are given, the essay might not flow or might seem disorganized. Finally, this question requires a precise writing plan with time to cover each directive subject; you would have to be especially careful not to run out of time and thus omit or superficially handle the final parts of this question or your essay would be incomplete.

Spotting the directive words and key words in your topic will help to get you over your first hurdle on a writing proficiency exam—or any other timed writing exam: what to write about. This step will also get you writing immediately and give you a sense of direction: these are important. Since your time is limited, you want to use every minute wisely. Analyzing your topic gets your ideas flowing and makes your brainstorming more effective.

Rule of Thumb #4: Begin writing immediately. Your brainstorming period is a time for thinking, but just as important, it is the time to begin writing—recording your thoughts as they come to you. Analyzing your exam question for directive and key words should take only two or three minutes; then you want to begin putting your thoughts on paper right away. Use these words in your exam question as your guide to keep your brainstorming focused (see Rule of Thumb #3).

Rule of Thumb #5: Construct an outline from your brainstorming notes to guide you in writing your draft. As you are recording ideas in your brainstorming, also consider the order, or sequence, in which you will present them. What point do you want to make? Do you want to build from least to most important? Will you follow a time sequence? Does *your topic* suggest some pattern or order for your paragraphs? Now you must plan a strategy for your essay by organizing your brainstorming information into a "scratch outline." This scratch outline is a tool for **you**: it helps you to envision both the content and structure of your essay. Use your directive words as **main headings** for your outline; key words could suggest **sub-headings**. (See Chapter 5 for more information on planning your essay.) An outline will also help you to formulate a clear thesis statement for your essay and a definite number of paragraphs you'll need to develop that thesis.[2] As your outline begins to take shape, work **with** it. **Don't waste time changing your mind!** Stick with the ideas you generated in your brainstorming.

DRAFTING AND CHECKING

Once your brainstorming is done and you have a scratch outline to guide you, you are ready to begin writing your draft. Plan to spend about three-fifths of your time drafting **and** revising[3] your draft (sixty to seventy-five minutes for a two-hour exam). Part of this time (perhaps five to ten minutes, after you have completed the draft) should be allotted for **checking** to see that you have focused on the question (answered all parts); written an introduction, body paragraphs and a conclusion; and used key words to unify your essay. Remember that you can make all these additions and changes on ONE draft; there is no need to write separate drafts with the changes—that could be unproductive and time-consuming. Do not worry about errors in spelling, punctuation, or grammar while you are drafting, revising, and checking. You may waste time correcting something that you might not use. You will have time to correct errors when you proofread.

---

[2]A **thesis** states the main point of your essay, the point that the paragraph unifying ideas will support. See Chapter 5 for a more thorough discussion of thesis.

[3]Here we use the term "revising" to refer to those changes you make *as you write*—crossing out words or substituting one word for another, crossing out or rewording sentences, crossing out parts of a paragraph you don't like and starting over: the kinds of changes you make as you change your mind while writing the draft. We refer to the more careful process of examining your draft for accuracy in content and structure as "checking."

Introduction

Rule of Thumb #6: Write an introductory paragraph that states your thesis and sets up body paragraphs. While your scratch outline is **your** blueprint for your essay, your readers will never see it. They, too, need to know what you are writing about, the stand you are taking, and the points you will make in your essay. Therefore, you give your readers a blueprint, or **road map** as we prefer to call it, in your introductory paragraph. (See Chapter 5 for more information on writing introductory paragraphs.) An introductory paragraph serves several important purposes in an essay; for one, it gets readers interested in what you have to say. But just as important, an introductory paragraph establishes your point of view and your plan to support your point. This set-up makes it easier for readers to follow and understand your essay. Therefore, begin your first draft by writing an introductory paragraph that clearly states your thesis and the main points you want to cover in the essay. Not only will an introductory paragraph help your readers; it will also help you: as you write your body paragraphs, you can refer to your introduction to make sure you are on track.

Unifying Ideas for Paragraphs

Rule of Thumb #7: Make sure each body paragraph has a unifying idea. On your scratch outline, you have grouped similar information together. These groups can now become the body paragraphs of your essay. Each group of information, or paragraph, must relate to your thesis; you express that relationship in a **unifying idea**.

A unifying idea, like a thesis statement, states a main idea you want to develop. The unifying idea is, however, narrower than the thesis statement; it focuses on one aspect of the thesis that will be developed **in a paragraph**. The unifying idea is a signal to both you **and** your readers; it tells what the paragraph is about and helps the reader make sense of your thoughts. Without a unifying idea, a paragraph is little more than a string of thoughts in the same space: readers may not understand the relationship among the thoughts by just reading them in sequence. A proficient writer demonstrates an understanding of paragraph structure by constructing each paragraph around a unifying idea and developing the paragraph with relevant support statements. A body paragraph should be about 6-10 sentences long.

Rule of Thumb #8: Avoid writing one-sentence or one-page paragraphs. A one-sentence paragraph lacks development; a one-page paragraph often rambles and lacks unity. Both are examples of nonproficient writing. Logic should tell you that one sentence cannot constitute a typical paragraph.[4] A one-sentence paragraph is more than likely a left-over thought that could more appropriately fit in another paragraph. Excessively long paragraphs are also a problem, although you may see them frequently in short stories and novels as well as textbooks. (William Faulkner and Henry James are two writers famous for their never-ending paragraphs.) Excessively long paragraphs can result from either failing to separate main ideas into individual paragraphs or providing too much information—some of which probably strays from the unifying idea. (Paragraph structure and development are discussed in detail in Chapters 4 and 6).

Conclusion and Checking

Rule of Thumb #9: Write a conclusion and check your essay for content and structure. Your conclusion can be the strongest part of your essay: it is an opportunity for you to restate your thesis, re-emphasize what you have said in your body paragraphs, and perhaps even shed new light on your main points. It is also *a chance for you to make a final positive impression on your reader*. (Writing conclusions is covered in Chapter 7.) In addition, readers expect some kind of "wind-up" so they will know when the writer is finished; abrupt endings can confuse or annoy them. Proficient writers give an essay a sense of completeness by writing a conclusion.

In a two-hour exam, your draft might be from three to five handwritten pages long, with approximately four to six paragraphs. When you have completed a draft, including writing your conclusion, your next step is **checking.**

---

[4]One-sentence paragraphs are not typical, but they may be used for special purposes in an essay. A writer may use a one-sentence statement between longer paragraphs to establish *transition*, or a link between the longer paragraphs. Or a writer may use a one-sentence paragraph for *emphasis*—to single out an important idea by physically separating it from longer paragraphs and giving the idea its own "paragraph." Use the one-sentence paragraph carefully and sparingly; if you have no specific reason for writing it, don't!

Checking is like revising, although you probably will have been actually revising—changing wording, adding or deleting details to sentences, and so forth—as you were writing your draft. Checking is an opportunity for you to enhance the content and structure of your essay as you read over your completed draft. After your draft is complete, you should be *checking* your essay for several features and taking a short time to make necessary changes or additions. Have you followed your outline in presenting your ideas? Could you add concrete examples to make a point more clear? Does each paragraph have a unifying idea? Can you reword a unifying idea to make it more relevant? Are there any awkwardly worded sentences that need rewording? Have you provided transitions within and between paragraphs to make your ideas flow? Does your essay focus clearly and thoroughly on the topic? As you read, you may find, for example, that you've stated your thesis more clearly in your conclusion than in your introduction or that you did not follow the sequence you presented in your introduction. Checking enables you to make changes in your essay that could mean the difference between passing and failing.

PROOFREADING

Rule of Thumb #10: Allow time to proofread your draft carefully for errors in grammar and mechanics. Though it is the last stage of your writing plan, proofreading is critical to proficiency. We form impressions about people based on many factors: appearance, manners, habits, attitudes, possessions. Did you ever think that your writing—especially the accuracy of your writing—also leads people to form an impression of you? Writing that is full of grammatical and mechanical errors gives readers an impression that the writer is careless and does not know—or perhaps does not care to apply—basic language rules. Consequently, careless writers are often judged as nonproficient. Therefore, it is important to allow time to proofread your essay for errors in grammar and mechanics.

The proofreading process should take up to one-fifth of your total time—10-25 minutes for a two-hour exam. Proofreading involves reviewing your draft for errors in grammar, usage, and mechanics. (Chapter 8 covers proofreading in more detail.) It is a *separate* process from checking. When you proofread, you are looking for different problems than when you read to check. You don't want to combine these two important tasks and perhaps slight one or the other. You'll be reading slowly and carefully, and making corrections as you read. Look for misspellings and awkward expressions. Make sure capital letters are distinguishable (especially if you print in all capitals), proper nouns (such as the titles of languages) are capitalized, and punctuation is at the end of each sentence. Also look for writing errors that *you* are prone to make—errors such as comma splices, incorrect pronoun references or agreements, fragments, or tense shifts. Instructors may have previously marked these on your papers. (Keeping a list of your most frequent errors, as discussed in Chapter 8, will help you to spot, correct, and—ultimately—overcome them.) You may want to proofread your draft more than once if you have time.

Also, **if you have time**, you can recopy your edited draft. However, simply spending time on neatness is wasteful; you can better use your time to make substantive changes and correct mistakes in your draft. Copying a draft is unnecessary *unless you are specifically instructed to do so*. In any timed writing exam, neatness is not a goal—writing a thorough, accurate, well-developed essay is. (If you are concerned about neatness, write on every other line as you write your draft; then you will have ample space to write in changes and corrections. Also, make deletions with a *single* cross-out line.) If you do have time to recopy, do so carefully. Often when students copy a draft in a hurry, they make mistakes—such as misspellings or omitted punctuation—that they don't normally make. Be sure not to leave out words—or even worse, entire lines! While you are copying, keep looking for errors and problems you may not have caught in proofreading.

EXERCISE 2-1

In the following writing proficiency exam topics, identify the key and directive words and tell how you would respond to those key and directive words in planning your essay.

TOPIC 1: Competition is built into many areas of American life: education, business, recreation. Discuss some of the positive and negative aspects of competition and analyze if the benefits balance the drawbacks.

TOPIC 2:. Everyone goes through ceremonies: graduations, award presentations, weddings, religious ceremonies. Some people look forward to such ceremonies; others regard them as expensive and unnecessary. Describe a ceremony you are familiar with and explain why you feel it is either worthwhile or not.

TOPIC 3: Specialists in education and child psychology do not agree upon the nature and extent of discipline—especially physical punishment—in raising children. Discuss the discipline you think is most appropriate and evaluate its effectiveness.

EXERCISE 2-2

Select one of the above topics and use the directive and key words to help you construct a scratch outline. You will have to add details suggested by the key and directive words. Pay careful attention to outline organization, or sequence of the ideas for the essay.

EXERCISE 2-3

Now determine the number of paragraphs your essay will have and write a unifying idea for each paragraph.

SUMMARY

Following the rules of thumb mentioned in this chapter will help you to form good writing habits and put you in control of your writing:

1. Have a plan for writing.
2. Allow time for brainstorming to generate and organize your ideas.
3. Identify the directive and key words in your exam question and use them to focus your brainstorming and formulate your essay.
4. Begin writing immediately.
5. Construct an outline from your brainstorming notes to guide you in writing your first draft.
6. Write an introductory paragraph that states your thesis and sets up body paragraphs.
7. Make sure each body paragraph has a unifying idea.
8. Avoid writing one-sentence or one-page paragraphs.
9. Write a conclusion and check your essay for content and structure.
10. Allow time to proofread your draft carefully for errors in grammar and mechanics.

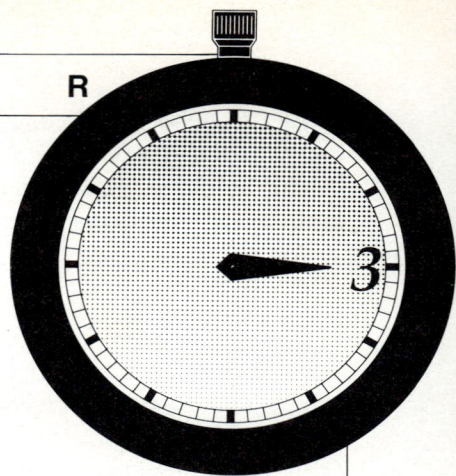

Generating Information Through Brainstorming

3

**USING CODE WORDS AS CLUES FOR IDEAS
CLUSTERING—"SEEING" WHAT YOU HAVE TO SAY
FREEWRITING—ANALYZING YOUR "FREE" THOUGHTS**

In Chapter 2—Taking a Timed Writing Exam: Rules of Thumb, you learned that an important strategy is to plan your time carefully. The first step of your plan, brainstorming, involves generating ideas and details for your essay.[1] Your brainstorming will help you discover what you have to say about your topic. Equally important, brainstorming will get you writing right away. Since your time is

---

[1]Generating ideas for an essay is sometimes called **pre-writing.** Pre-writing, however, may suggest activities that occur *before* you actually begin to write. Thus, we prefer to call the information generating phase of the writing process "**brainstorming**," because you will be *writing* as well as thinking.

limited, you don't want to waste any of it staring at a blank piece of paper. You want to quickly fill that paper with thoughts that you will eventually turn into a thesis, unifying ideas, and support statements for your paragraphs. This chapter presents practical approaches to generating ideas and starting the writing process. Though there are many brainstorming techniques, the ones mentioned here—using code words, clustering, and freewriting—will help you to generate useful, relevant information **quickly**, since your time for brainstorming is limited. These techniques will also help you to sort out your thoughts and eliminate ineffective ideas early in the writing process, so you won't waste time on unproductive responses in your drafting stage.

Brainstorming is a method of generating and developing ideas by association—a process in which one thought leads to another, and you write down these thoughts as they come to you. When you brainstorm, you are *discovering* what you want to say—you may not really know yet. You let your thoughts flow to uncover your impressions. To an extent, brainstorming is an "anything goes" process. You should write down everything you think of, as long as you don't stray from your topic (you can always eliminate weak ideas later).

The brainstorming process is probably not new to you. As chair of a club's fundraising committee, you may have had brainstorming sessions with committee members to come up with ideas for fundraising activities. On your job, you may have participated in a staff brainstorming session to find ways of improving employee performance. Or on a Friday night, you may have sat around with your friends deliberating which party to attend or what movie to see. In these situations, you are expressing various ideas and examining possibilities and options. At some point in the process, you will eliminate what isn't feasible or desirable, and expand upon the remaining ideas. For example, in your Friday night brainstorming session, you and your friends may eliminate parties and decide to go to a movie; you'll then brainstorm on which movie to see. You may use the various movie categories—such as drama, comedy, musical, mystery, or science fiction—to help you think of possibilities. Your brainstorming helps to uncover everyone's ideas and feelings, and ultimately to make a decision.

On a proficiency exam (or in any other timed writing situation), your brainstorming period will be limited, but it is critical to organizing your ideas and developing your essay thoroughly. Thus, focusing on your topic immediately is important to your success.

Three brainstorming techniques useful in generating specific information rapidly are *using code words*, *clustering*, and *freewriting*.

USING CODE WORDS AS CLUES FOR IDEAS

As mentioned in Chapter 2, your exam question will give you clues as to how to formulate your response. You should first identify *directive words* in the topic or question that will give you a general idea of what you should cover and approximately how many paragraphs you should write. Then read your topic carefully for *code words*, or more specific *key words* that suggest particular ideas, points of view, beliefs or experiences. (Chapter 2—Rule of Thumb #3 discusses identifying and using directive and key words.) Use these code words to get your thoughts flowing. Brainstorming with code words is a process of association: a code word from your exam question helps you think of a specific word from your experience or knowledge, which helps you recall a pertinent incident, and so forth. Brainstorming with code words from the question keeps you organized: the list of words and phrases you write down for each code word can become a paragraph. In addition, brainstorming with code words will help you to more thoroughly address your question: each code word will suggest a different aspect of your response for which you'll generate ideas. Your code words will also help keep you focused on the question, so though your brainstorming may be spontaneous, it is not random. For example, note the code words in the following topic and how they can be used in brainstorming. First read the essay topic; then write down the underlined code words and the words or phrases that come to your mind as you think about each code word.

> *Topic:* Whether your parents or guardians were permissive or strict, they undoubtedly disciplined you in some way. Describe their disciplinary practices as you were growing up and explain the effects that their discipline had on you. Then discuss how your parents' disciplinary practices influence (or will influence) you as a parent disciplining your children.

(Note **directive words:** describe, explain, discuss)

Code words: disciplinary practices   effects
                                                          influence (on me)

Now compare your code word lists to the following lists one writer made to generate ideas for the discipline essay.

Disciplinary Practices

spanking   anger   yelling   harsh   severe   belt
restrictions   no T.V.   no phone calls   missed parties
no friends over   missed jr. prom   had to do chores or
else   no "privileges"   couldn't use car   slapping
spanking   old-fashioned   inconsistent   never knew
what to expect   hostility

Effects

fear   anger   resentment   unhappy   felt unloved
thought parents were mean   got good grades   respect
afraid   cooperation   distance   not close w/dad then
or now   hostility   obey laws   responsible
respect authority   no rebellion

Influence

more understanding   will NOT spank   patience
restrictions   set limits   be calm   love
communicate   be reasonable   deny privileges
be consistent   no yelling

This brainstorming session, which took the writer only ten minutes, yielded a variety of important details and facts. Each list of words/phrases could turn into a paragraph, and the words/phrases in each list suggest an overall impression which could be expressed in a unifying idea or topic sentence. For example, under the *disciplinary practices* list, we see that the writer's discipline included spankings, restrictions and denial of privileges; this system of parental discipline, he feels, was quite harsh. The writer could turn his notion into this unifying idea:

> My parents' disciplinary practices were unnecessarily harsh; to punish me, they spanked me and denied me privileges or created restrictions for even the slightest infractions of their rules.

To support this unifying idea, the writer could elaborate on the spankings (**belt**, **slapping**), the restrictions (**missed parties** and

junior prom, no phone calls) and the denied privileges **(couldn't use car, no T.V., no friends over)**. He could also discuss the reason for the harsh discipline **(old-fashioned)**, the inconsistency of his discipline and the negative feelings that accompanied it **(yelling, anger, hostility)**. The information he generated through this brainstorming is vivid, concrete, and thoroughly addresses the first part of his topic: "Describe their disciplinary practices as you were growing up."

The writer could easily develop paragraphs from his code word lists for *effects* and *influence*. His *effects* list suggests that he resented his parents, but learned to respect authority (though probably out of fear); his *influences* list suggests that though he is more patient and understanding as a parent, he uses some of the same disciplinary practices his parents used (**denial** and **restrictions**).

His ten-minute brainstorming session generated pertinent, well organized information for his entire essay because he used code words from his topic to get him started. In developing his essay, he could also echo his code words—repeat them to keep both himself and his reader on track.

CLUSTERING—SEEING WHAT YOU HAVE TO SAY

Another method of brainstorming is *clustering*. Like code word brainstorming, you begin clustering by identifying key words or ideas in your exam topic or question. However, unlike code word brainstorming which requires you to consider only one key word at a time as you generate thoughts, clustering allows you to jump from one key word to another as different thoughts come to your mind. Thus clustering is a process of categorizing similar thoughts. As each thought comes to mind, you write it down with a group (or cluster) of corresponding ideas that relate to a key word (see Figure 1). This process is also called "treeing": a main thought (suggested by a key or directive word in your exam topic or question) becomes the "trunk" of the tree, and other related thoughts are "branches." Clustering is a good visual method of generating ideas—you can actually see your essay's paragraphs begin to take shape in the clusters of ideas you record.

Clustering enables you to respond to your topic as a whole, rather than to each part separately. In doing so, there is less chance of your "losing" an important thought because you are not yet brainstorming for that information. For example, as you read the topic on discipline, the first thought that comes to your mind may be, "My parents were really tough and sometimes unreasonable." This thought could begin a cluster of similar thoughts—"frequent spankings," "quick to get angry at small infractions of the rules," "never listened to my side of the story." After writing down this last thought, you may think, "When I become a parent, I am going to listen to my children." This new thought will begin a cluster of ideas about how your parents' discipline will affect your parenting methods. Your next thought may deal with the effects of your parents' discipline, which will start a new cluster: "resentment," "fear," "false respect for authority." But then you may think, "I remember how my dad forced me to call him 'sir' to show my respect." So that thought will go in your very first cluster on "tough and unreasonable." Thus, though you may be thinking at random, you are recording your thoughts in an orderly way.

At the end of your brainstorming period, you will have several clusters of information, each of which was prompted by your topic and could be developed into a paragraph, just as in code word brainstorming. Each cluster will deal with a different aspect of your topic and will suggest an overall impression that you can turn into a unifying idea. In addition, you may have written down some of your thoughts in sentence form rather than in single words; these sentences can be more easily integrated into paragraphs.

One method of clustering the ideas generated by brainstorming is shown in Figure 1.

FREEWRITING

Freewriting is an aid to discovery and thus a form of brainstorming, but it uses a different format. Although you use key words from your exam question to get your freewriting started, you record your thoughts in a continuous stream, in sentence-like statements, rather than in lists or clusters of words and phrases. Freewriting is exactly that—free. Though the statements you write may look like sentences, you need not be concerned with correct spelling, grammar, punctuation, mechanics, or any writing rules. You are simply discovering what you have to say, and you don't want rules to get in the way of your thoughts. Just write down whatever comes to your mind, and watch your ideas unfold as you write. The three important guidelines for freewriting are: write down *everything* you think of; keep your pen moving for the entire freewriting period—

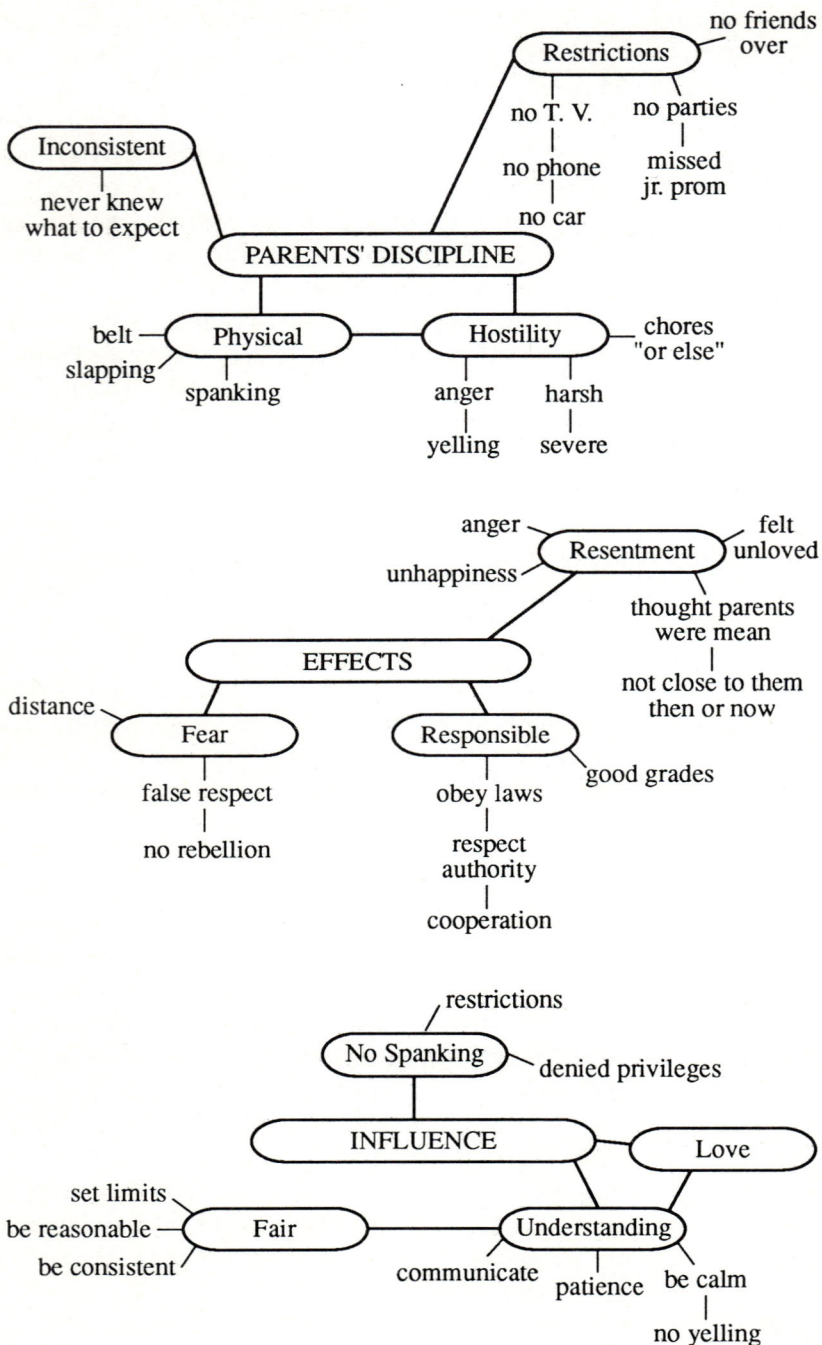

Figure 1

don't stop writing; try not to look back—don't stop to read over what you have written because you may lose your train of thought (and you will not be writing if you stop to read).

Freewriting is an especially good method of generating ideas when you feel you have *absolutely nothing* to write about, when a topic frustrates you, or when you are blocking on a topic (you may have some ideas but don't know how to express them). In these instances you may approach freewriting by writing about *why* you can't write about a topic. Since you are not bound by rules and formats and can write down anything you want, you may feel more comfortable with writing and your ideas will flow much more easily. In particular, freewriting can get you started writing quickly. Of course you will have to take time later to organize your ideas, but you will not be wasting time staring at a blank piece of paper.

Here is an example of how a student (who was reluctant to write about the discipline topic) generated ideas for her essay through freewriting:

> I am a college senior and they ask me to write about discipline—what a joke. Youd think I was six years old. This is really dumb, who wants to write about their disiplin anyway—not me. I dont even like to think about it no less write about it. My parents were terrors—I mean, I love them today and all, and I know they thought they were doing the best thing for me, but wow! sometimes they were so mean! I mean heres this poor little helpless kid and every time I turn around I'm doing something wrong! Don't do this. Don't do that. No T.V. No friends over. No dessert. Go to your room. You can't play until you've "thought about" what you did. Who wants to think when they're a kid? Well, I suppose it could have been worse. They could of spanked me. And maybe that would have been better, actually. One swift spanking and that's it. But nooooooo! I had to THINK ABOUT what I did. And sometimes I even had to make up my own punishments! That's a real heavy trip to lay on an eight year old who didn't think there was anything wrong with saying shut up to her sister in the first place. Sometimes I get really angry when I remember those quiet talks about how bad I was—what a wretched child I was. Talk about no self-confidence. I grew up thinking that everything bad was my fault. There's got to be a better way, and I'll find it

for my own kids. Maybe it is spankings—but not with anger. Maybe it is no T.V. But it sure ain't THINKING!!!!

Through these very candid thoughts, this student has generated a wealth of information for her essay. She has a thesis: Though her parents refrained from corporal punishment, their disciplinary practices were harsh because they expected a young child to be logical and rational about misbehaving **(They were terrors. They were really mean. I had to THINK about what I did)**. She cites specific punishments she endured **(no T.V., no friends over, no dessert, go to your room and think)** and she mentions a particular discipline tactic that bothered her **(sometimes I had to make up my own punishments)** to support her thesis. She even gives an example of how her parents' logic in discipline escaped her as a child **(she did not think saying shut up to her sister was wrong)**. In addition, she analyzes how their discipline affected her **(Talk about no self-confidence. I grew up thinking everything bad was my fault.)** Finally, she speculates on how she will discipline her children in light of the discipline she received **(Maybe it's spankings. Maybe it's no T.V. But it sure ain't THINKING!)**. Furthermore, she could easily and quickly turn these rough notes into a scratch outline, which would help her organize her ideas and establish a sequence for her essay (see Figure 2).

Though she expresses her ideas in a very raw form and with a number of mechanical errors (which is acceptable for freewriting), she has addressed all parts of the discipline topic. As she writes, revises, and proofreads her actual essay, she will formulate paragraphs from her raw thoughts, develop her ideas more thoroughly, and correct her grammatical and mechanical errors. Through her freewriting, she has uncovered pertinent thoughts on a topic she originally felt she could not write on.

Discovering what you have to say about a topic by freewriting, clustering or code word brainstorming can help you get your thoughts flowing. Think of them as a kind of "research"—you are searching your own mind to uncover your ideas. You may want to experiment with the three brainstorming methods to find the one that works best for you, then use that one method all the time. Or you may find that different topics require different brainstorming methods, and you will select an appropriate technique for each individual writing task or topic. But remember, regardless of the amount of time you have to write your essay or exam, devote at least a few minutes to this important idea-discovery stage.

I am a college senior and they ask me to write about discipline–what a joke. You'd think I was six years old. This is really dumb, who wants to write about their discipline anyway–not me. I don't even like to think about it no less write about it. **Thesis?** (My parents were terrors) I mean, I love them today and all, and I know they thought they were doing the best thing for me, but wow! Sometimes (they were so mean!) I mean here's this poor little helpless kid and every time I turn around I'm doing something wrong! Don't do **Examples** this. Don't do that. (No T.V) (No friends over.) (No dessert) (Go to your room) You can't play until you've "thought about" what you did. Who wants to think when they're a kid? Well, I suppose it could have been worse. They could of spanked me. And maybe that would have been better, actually. One **Too Logical** swift spanking and that's it. But nooooooo! (I had to THINK ABOUT what I did) And sometimes I even **unfair** had to (make up my own punishments) That's a real heavy trip to lay on an eight year old who didn't think **Example** there was (anything wrong with saying shut up to her) sister in the first place. Sometimes (I get really angry) when I remember those quiet talks about how bad I **Effects** was–what a wretched child I was. Talk about (no self-confidence) I grew up (thinking that everything bad was my fault.) There's got to be a better way, and I'll **Me as** find it for my own kids. Maybe it is (spankings–but **a parent** not with anger) Maybe it is (no T.V) But it sure (ain't THINKING!!!)

I. Parents Were Mean
   A. Frequent Punishments—no TV, no dessert, no friends over, stay in room
   B. Too Logical
      1. made me "think" about what I did wrong
      2. I didn't understand their logic
         a. shut up to sister wasn't bad to me
      3. I had to make up my own punishments

II. Today I Resent Their Discipline
   A. Memories Make Me Mad
   B. Discipline Caused No Self-Confidence
      1. Thought everything I did was wrong

III. I Will Be Different As A Parent
   A. Spankings?? No Anger
   B. Denied Privileges—No TV
   C. No Thinking—Tangible Punishments

Figure 2

EXERCISE 3-1

Spend no more than 10 minutes brainstorming on the following topic. First, identify directive and key words in the question. Use either the *code word* or the *clustering* approach. When you are done with your brainstorming, examine your lists or clusters of thoughts and write a unifying idea for each which could be supported with the ideas in the list/cluster.

TOPIC: Discuss an event that was a turning point in your life. Describe what your life was like before the event, and analyze the changes that took place in your life because of the event. Then evaluate what you learned from your experience.

EXERCISE 3-2

Freewrite for 10 minutes on the following topic. Write down everything that you think of and *do not stop writing for the full 10 minutes.* Then read over your freewriting and look for a main idea that you could turn into a thesis and sub-ideas that could be unifying ideas for paragraphs. Write your thesis and unifying ideas. Then look for statements and examples that you could use to support your unifying ideas, and list them under each unifying idea.

TOPIC: Analyze a time when you and another person had a strong difference in opinion over an issue. Explain both your point of view and the other person's beliefs, and evaluate whether or not your examination of *both* sides could help *you* reach a resolution or greater understanding.

SUMMARY

1. After reading your exam question, spend some time brainstorming. Brainstorming can help you quickly discover what you want to say about a topic.
2. Some topics are most easily developed using code words—a logical, structured approach of listing words and phrases that relate to key words from your topic.
3. The clustering approach enables you to "see" your thoughts and quickly organize them in groups of similar ideas as you think about what you want to write.

4. If you feel you have nothing at all to say on a topic, try freewriting for a short period of time to unlock your thoughts.
5. Brainstorming can develop possible responses to an essay question or topic and can generate details that you will flesh out in your essay draft. It can also help you eliminate unproductive ideas before you actually begin writing your essay.

4

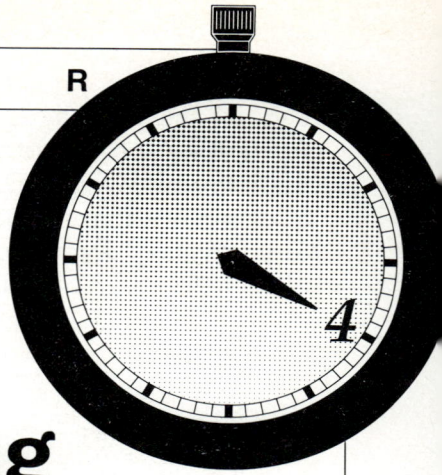

Paragraphing Proficiently

Once you have generated ideas in response to the topic, you can begin writing your essay. The building blocks of an essay are paragraphs. In fact, the paragraph is the primary **unit of thought**— or way of organizing experience—in writing. Because of this principle of unity, proficient paragraphs can be constructed by unifying each paragraph with a single idea, concept, or insight. By dividing your essay into paragraphs, you help your reader to see the structure of your thinking. The visual cue is simple, maybe even subtle—a small indentation at the beginning of the paragraph, empty space after the end of its final sentence.[1] That's just enough for a good reader to take a breather, or to find the place again after a pause.

If you fail to paragraph, you offer the reader a kind of chaos—four to five pages of writing without any indentations, any breaks, any pauses, any clues to idea structure. It would be one undifferentiated clump—as hard to digest intellectually as a 1-inch uncut sirloin steak would be hard to digest physically. Imagine reading a whole book (200–400 pages) without a single indentation. That would be a daunting experience! And that was why the paragraph was invented—to provide useful cues and breaks for the reader in understanding your ideas.

If you wrote a long composition without paragraphs, that would annoy and disconcert many readers. By the same token, if you used paragraphs but inserted them arbitrarily, you would provide the wrong cues to your reader. If every paragraph were simply a single sentence, the paragraph would fail to organize your thinking in any useful way.[2] Thus a good rule of thumb (as mentioned in Chapter 2, Taking a Timed Writing Exam: Rules of Thumb) to follow is to avoid one-page paragraphs and one-sentence paragraphs. Proficient paragraphs tend to have four to ten sentences.

UNIFYING IDEA

But of just what is a paragraph composed? Of a unifying idea and a variety of relevant support for that idea. That support often consists of definition, explanation, clarification, and—especially—concrete examples. The **unifying idea** is the term we use—reminding you that proficient essays consist of a group of concentric units: whole essay, paragraph, sentence. You may be familiar with the unifying

---

[1]Some formats, particularly in business, don't use indentations. However, if you are writing in longhand, or in a hurry, it's important to leave that space (maybe half an inch) at the beginning so that the reader has no doubt a new paragraph has begun. Leaving a barely perceptible space or no space at all will confuse and annoy a reader.

[2]Many of you will have noticed that newspapers are often filled with one-sentence paragraphs. This is a convention of journalism—where printing in columns can make single sentences quite long. A journalistic article is primarily a list of facts, rather than an exposition or explanation of ideas. You might notice that paragraphs in Sunday opinion sections conform more closely to the principles we suggest here.

idea as the topic sentence. Or perhaps it has been called the "controlling idea" or the "paragraph-idea" or the "central idea." But call it what you will, it is the same piece of reasoning—a sentence which alerts the reader to the subject of your paragraph, that "contracts" with the reader to provide evidence on or explanation of a particular topic. Thus a paragraph which does not *develop* this idea fails because it does not prove or support its point. Also a paragraph which attempts to develop the unifying idea *and other ideas,* too, fails because it confuses your reader. A unifying idea consists of one subject and a point of view or attitude toward that subject.

Before going any further, it will help to examine two examples of proficient paragraphs. (Unifying ideas appear in **boldface** and are underlined. When you are writing your draft, you might improve your writing and keep your idea clearly in mind by underlining the unifying idea for each paragraph.)

A   Recently a new fad has appeared in California fashion: stone-washed denim fabric. This fad can be recognized by the hue of the denim—it has been washed in a solution of acid which streaks the ordinarily blue jeans with shades of white and dark. This fad is apparent in pants, jackets, purses, jewelry, shirts, socks, shoes, and whatever else the manufacturer thinks of. I first recognized the mania for stone-washed fabrics in fall 1987 at a fashion show in San Francisco. Twenty of the thirty models wore at least one piece of stone-washed fabric; I even saw a male modeling a stone-washed tie. At that time I realized that stone-washed clothing was the latest California fad. Now even I wear the style.

B   **In the mid 1980s American business leaders have become alarmed by the lack of communication skills in the young people they employ.** Recently, top executives of some large U.S. companies, including CBS and Exxon, met to discuss the fact that their younger middle-level executives could no longer communicate their ideas effectively in speech or writing. This group of companies has made a grant to the American Academy of Arts and Sciences to analyze the causes of this growing problem. They want to know why, despite breathtaking advances in the technology of communication, the effectiveness of business communication has been slipping, to the detriment of our competitiveness in the world. The figures from National Assessment of Educational Progress (NAEP) surveys and the scores on the verbal Scholastic Aptitude Test (SAT) are solid evidence that literacy has been declining in this country just when our need for effective literacy has been sharply rising.[3]

Notice how each unifying idea governs its paragraph. In paragraph A, the first sentence states both subject (stone-washed fabric) and attitude or judgment (it is a recent California fad). The other six sentences in the paragraph offer more specific information to define and describe "stone-washed jeans" and to show that they have recently become popular in a variety of forms. You should notice that none of the sentences is about another topic, such as what else the author did in San Francisco in 1987, her other clothing preferences, or the properties of acid. The writer keeps the paragraph in focus.

In paragraph B, the unifying idea identifies the subject (lack of communication skills) and the judgment (alarm of business executives over this trend). The other four sentences in the paragraph offer more specific information (which companies, for example) and evidence of the declining skills in communication (such as the NAEP surveys or the SAT scores). The remainder of the paragraph also explains why businesses are concerned (declining literacy makes them less competitive). Notice how Hirsch doesn't stray from his subject either—he doesn't write about Japanese competition, or CBS's problem with corporate takeovers, or the drug epidemic in the schools, or any other idea not directly developing his topic.

Although a unifying idea or topic sentence can appear anywhere in a paragraph (second sentence, a middle sentence, final sentence)[4], typically it comes first. Why? It helps to prepare readers so they can see how the information that follows fits together. It also helps guide you as the writer, because it implicitly sets up a plan

---

[3]E.D. Hirsch, Jr., *Cultural Literacy* (New York: Random House, 1988), 5.

[4]Writers may make a second sentence the unifying idea because the first sentence is merely introductory, setting a particular time and place. Writers may locate a unifying idea in the midst or at the end of a paragraph to give a reader a sense of discovery, or create some suspense or mystery. But when you are writing under time pressure, it's hard to unify the paragraph effectively with these other techniques.

and purpose for what you will write. Because you are under time pressure on exams, you will usually write more proficiently if you *begin* paragraphs with a unifying idea.

UNIFYING IDEA: JUDGMENT OR FACT?

Notice also that a unifying idea is an opinion, judgment or generalization. Why? It leaves certain terms or issues unclear or unstated so that the rest of the paragraph can develop these through explanation or example. Sentences which are narrow facts fail to unify paragraphs and usually lead writers astray into irrelevance or confusion. Consider the following sentences:

1. This sentence ends with a period.
2. When I was 18, I entered college, took 15 units of classes, and worked 40 hours a week.
3. I was married to a woman whose name was Eleanor.
4. When I received an A in my English class, I was shocked.
5. This paragraph is about guns.

None of these sentences provides an effective unifying idea for a paragraph because each is a self-contained fact. The reader cannot argue with it or doubt it or expect it to be explained, defined, or supported. Usually sentences like these evade or mask an idea that a writer really does wish to develop. They often name a subject or refer to a topic area (punctuation, overwork, romance, educational injustice, guns), but *avoid a judgment*. Sometimes the **writer** knows the attitude he or she wishes to develop, but the reader can only guess—and often the paragraph goes astray as a result. Perhaps the implied unifying idea behind (2.) is that the writer was unprepared for college, misallocated her time, and learned painfully from the experience. Perhaps the writer in (3.) wants to examine why he was attracted to his wife, or how the marriage mixed bliss and suffering, or that his wife's name offered symbolic insight into her character. The masked topic of (4.) consists, most likely, of the *reasons* why the writer was shocked. Even the shock, though an emotion, is inarguable by a reader and must be accepted as fact. In all these cases the writer has not done the work a writer should: the writer has left all the work up to the reader's ingenuity and imagination. But most readers of expository prose resent such an approach.

Proficient unifying ideas offer judgments by using evaluative words—for example: "good," "misleading," "indifferent," "disappointing," "advantageous"—or by suggesting how a topic may be usefully subdivided: "long-lasting love is determined by three qualities: commitment, passion, and intimacy." Typically, a unifying idea involves some abstraction—a quality that cannot be determined by sight, hearing, touch, taste, or feel.

NARROWING THE UNIFYING IDEA

Some unifying ideas are not proficient because they are not judgments, but facts, and thus provide the reader with little guidance, and the writer with no plan for development. Other unifying ideas are not proficient because they are too broad or general and simply cannot be developed within the scope of a paragraph. Overgeneralization characterizes the following test unifying ideas:

1. There are all kinds of people in the world.
2. I experienced a variety of problems.
3. My experience of higher education was difficult.

In order to narrow a sentence like one of these, try writing a second sentence that follows from the first, but is more specific. Ask yourself narrowing questions such as "which kinds of people are critical?" or "when, where, and how did I experience these problems?"; "which problems?"; "in what subject did I have the most difficulty and why?" Questions like these could lead to replacements for the test ideas such as the following:

R1. Strong-willed people conflict with those who are more passive.
R2. When I was a teenager, a cast on my leg confronted me with problems in transportation, unwanted pity, and bathing.
R3. Because I did not develop effective studying methods for finals, I failed my math course in college.

A unifying idea works if it is broad enough to control the information offered in the paragraph and yet narrow enough to give direction to the writer and reader. In other words, you ought to be able to relate directly and clearly **every** sentence in your paragraph to your unifying idea. In this way, the unifying idea **controls** the information. Also, it shouldn't be so broad that it could function in virtually any paragraph—that it relates vaguely to wide varieties of other ideas or facts. If your unifying idea satisfies these demands, it is sufficiently **narrow.** If the paragraph offers information extraneous to its unifying idea, either the sentence expressing the idea should be rewritten, or the extraneous material should be cut.

The following paragraphs are flawed because of weak unifying ideas. Perhaps some sentences fail to support the idea. Or perhaps there is no idea — merely several statements of fact. Or perhaps the idea is too broad and the paragraph goes off in a number of directions.

Example A

During my sophomore year at State College, I enrolled in a German class with Amy Forge, a part-time instructor. Amy was always on time, began the class by offering us a detailed syllabus, and never humiliated a single student during the entire semester. Once she even brought pictures of her children. I thought she was a great instructor because she was from Germany and brought many of her experiences to class. Learning a different language is very hard because the different grammar, structure and pronunciation all present problems. If Professor Forge had taught directly from the book, the class would have been boring; but assignments asking us to compare cultures (school system and traditional festivals) made the class compelling and exciting. Professor Forge explained that schools in Europe were harder on the high school level than the high schools in the United States. Schools in Germany were in session 6 days a week with only two months off for summer vacation. She also explained that at the end of high school, students were required to pass a certain test. If the students did not pass, then they did not graduate. Compared to our schools here in the United States, German high schools are more tedious and stressful; I am glad to have attended high school here in the U.S. Professor Forge also explained that the German people are very festive and enjoy preserving ancient traditions. The annual Oktoberfest is one such festival: it celebrates harvest time. The fest goes on for days; the Germans dress in the traditional lederhosen and dirndl for the occasion. They also drink, eat, and dance merrily. I thought that was wonderful how whole towns can get together and enjoy themselves. There is nothing in the United States that does that except for the German communities who put on their own Oktoberfest. So in this class, I learned about the vocabulary and grammar as well as the different lifestyle Germans have because my instructor was so familiar with German culture. An interesting note is that Americans have picked up words from the Germans and used them here. For instance, take the word "kindergarten"—there is no other word that can be used in place of it.

Though it has a unifying idea (the class might have been boring, but assignments on comparative cultures made it exciting), the paragraph contains much distracting information, such as the comments about the personality of the professor, the writer's editorializing about life in the United States, and the anticlimactic information about *kindergarten*. **Narrowing the unifying idea and omitting irrelevant information would make the paragraph proficient.**

Example B

In June 1985 I enrolled in an American History class taught by Professor Cary. Professor Cary always came to class dressed in a bow tie, sport coat, and wing-tips. Professor Cary had three degrees from Harvard and talked with a distinct Boston accent. His behavior in class was often odd. Once, when a dog barked endlessly outside the classroom during a lecture, Professor Cary barked in imitation of the dog; finally, it quit. Professor Cary's view of the depression and World War II was critical of President Roosevelt for not following through on the essentially socialist course he was pursuing in the New Deal. The class ended with an excellent party; everyone got drunk and Professor Cary even took off his bow tie.

Though not as long as the paragraph on the German instructor, this paragraph wanders and confuses the reader because it begins with a statement of *fact* rather than a *unifying idea*. The paragraph could be improved by *adding* a unifying idea as the second sentence: "Professor Cary was never as formal or distant as he first seemed; both his demeanor in class and his intellectual approach to history revealed he cared for the common people and an ordinary good time."

Example C

> The woman's movement poses serious problems for the sensitive male in dating, creating a quandary at every step of the relationship. The sensitive male wonders if he should call her for a date, or wait for her to make the first move. If he does make a date, should he offer to drive, or suggest that she pick him up? If he does drive and arrives at her house, perhaps he is in a quandary as to whether to open her car door or allow her to perform that act herself. He worries, too, about who should pay for dinner. Even at the end of the evening, he is stuck, confused—should he kiss her good-night or expect her to make the first move? It's a wonder in the era of the women's movement that the sensitive male even dates at all.

The first sentence in Example C is the unifying idea. Note how it makes a judgment, open to question, about dating. Note also how "problems" and "quandary" are borne out by the series of issues about which the male wonders, worries over, or questions. Thus the first sentence narrows, guides, and unifies the paragraph. And each of the following sentences relates directly to that first sentence, creating a sense of unity.

METHODS OF DEVELOPING THE UNIFYING IDEA:

Using Concrete Details

A paragraph consists not only of a unifying idea, but also of development for that idea. This is one of the reasons a good paragraph is usually longer than a single sentence. You can support your unifying idea by a variety of methods—by defining and explaining, by offering examples, by comparisons, by arguments. Usually the most effective method on an exam is to generate concrete details. What is concrete? Often students are instructed to create concreteness by providing sensory detail: sight, sound, touch, taste, smell. But a good test to see if your development is concrete is to ask if this is an event or experience that happened at one time, at one place only. Study the following examples; they progressively narrow the topic and add concreteness:

English was always my worst subject. [Too broad, this happened many times over a period of years.]

English was my worst subject in college. I failed English once, and the other times I took a course in it, my grades were not good. I never enjoyed it and I never understood it. Each writing assignment was a disaster. [Narrower, but this still doesn't give a reader much sense of why this writer felt English was his worst subject. Though it narrows the topic at least to the college years, the following sentences are still quite vague and general.]

English was my worst subject my freshman year in college. For example, I remember one essay my English professor returned to me the second week of my freshman composition course. There was a red splotch or scribble that seemed to begin in my first paragraph and seep slowly through the essay until it reached my conclusion. The professor had written a short essay of her own at the end commenting on my ignorance of the paragraph, my comma faults, and my failure to develop an idea in any detail. Unfortunately, this essay typified my performance in the class. [Now the paragraph development is concrete—because the experience used as an example happened only once. And the development shows the reader you remember your difficulty with composition clearly and vividly. Perhaps the paragraph evokes similar experiences the reader may have shared.]

Without some concrete detail, your paragraph will often appear general and vague and offer no more than what seems obvious to most readers. Proficient writing, though, consists of offering readers what they don't know or don't think they know. Good development of a paragraph offers "proof" of your idea for a reader. Of course, outside of self-contained mathematical systems, or the piling up of statistical evidence, no writer offers the kind of proof that is inarguable. Nor would you merely want to offer dry statistics. Instead, you offer representative examples, details that characterize your idea so that a reader can identify with your experience and thinking, and affirm or sympathize with your judgment. Even if a reader doesn't agree, the example makes your point clearly and forcefully.

Quite often an essay is not proficient because paragraphs lack sufficient or convincing detail. In fact, we find most writing that fails to be proficient fails because it is poorly developed—because paragraphs consist of three to five sentences, each of which is a generalization or abstraction. Take the following paragraph, for example:

Version A

Decades ago, women were not allowed to go to school or pursue careers. The women's movement changed that; and women now go on to college and graduate school; and many are entering the professions. Women see more to their lives now than just being wives and mothers.

Though the paragraph is clear and makes sense, it consists almost entirely of generalizations. A generalization covers a wide body of information and experience, and usually makes a broad claim. Yet the paragraph does not advance much in conception beyond the idea that women are now going to school. This paragraph is broad, vague, bland and true. There is very little here for an educated reader to argue with, but that does not make the paragraph proficient. Now examine a revised version of that paragraph, improved by use of concrete detail.

Version B

In the nineteenth century women rarely went beyond high school and rarely considered work outside the home. They were seen only as wives and mothers by men who thought, "they do not need to go to school." The women's movement, maturing in the 1920s and accelerating in the 1970s, changed that; now in 1988 women are not just graduating from high school but going beyond, to college and often graduate school. Over 50% of my classes here at the University of Texas are populated by women. I see numbers of women in my accounting classes. For example, my friend Alice is taking Cost Accounting and plans to become a comptroller for a local corporation; but Alice's mother is a housewife who never went beyond high school. An acquaintance of ours, June, is taking courses in organic chemistry and planning to apply for medical school. Fifty years ago she would have considered only nursing and would not have gone to college. Clearly, women see more to their lives now than just being wives and mothers; they also consider entering professions, just as men do.

Notice that the examples of Alice and June are concrete—they are individuals who exist at a particular point in space and time. Using them helps to bring the paragraph down to earth from a cloudy level of generalization. You might also notice that the revised paragraph is considerably longer, but it is not longer because it is wordy, repetitious, or stuffed with filler. The details are related to the unifying idea and convince the reader of its value.

Using Topics of Invention

How do writers develop a unifying idea when all they have is a bare skeleton of an outline or several words and phrases developed in brainstorming? They often use the **topics of invention**— that is, they ask themselves questions that prompt added information. These questions are themselves a form of brainstorming: they can be used to generate the data for an entire essay. They are particularly appropriate in developing or revising paragraphs. These are the questions proficient writers ask:

- **Who?** Who did it? Who is responsible? Who is a prominent example of the phenomenon I am describing? Can I name a person that is involved?

- **What?** What is the subject? What is the problem? What is the issue or the theory?

- **Where?** Where did this event or this cultural movement take place? In what country or city or state or college or street or room or field or apartment building or barn?

- **When?** When did this event or cultural movement take place? At what date or time? At what crucial period of my life, such as just after my high school graduation, just before my recent divorce, the moment I finally understood the grammar of German? Was it at the time of any other important event that readers could identify with, such as the invention of moveable type, the presidential campaign of 1968, the great San Francisco earthquake?

- **Why?** Why did this occur? What are its causes? What principle or theory or behavior led to these results? Is there any explanation for this phenomenon, process or event? Why did I say what I did? Why do I hold this opinion or take this stand?

- **How?** In what manner or by what process did this occur? What were the key ingredients? What were the key steps? How can the issue be resolved? How did the problem arise?

- **Can I offer an example?** Is there an instance of this phenomenon known to me from my reading, observation, or direct experience? Is there an anecdote that can illustrate my point?

You need not memorize these topics, or use each one every time, but you could keep using them after *every* sentence in a paragraph in order to develop it effectively. Let us illustrate by beginning with a paragraph that is underdeveloped, that is a bare skeleton:

Version A

1
     Dr. Alanson, the professor in my Introduction to Psychology class at West Powhatan College, had many
2   outstanding qualities. Dr. Alanson was distinguished by his
3   integrity and intensity. If Dr. Alanson saw a wrong being
4   committed, he didn't turn and look away. Dr. Alanson worked hard at living life to the fullest.

Though this paragraph is clear and readable, it lacks conviction because there are *no details*. In fact, it is only the skeleton of a proficient paragraph.

Let us see how we can use topics of invention to develop this paragraph effectively and make it exciting for a reader. Using the topics of invention is primarily a mental process; you do not need to write the process down. Instead, write down and combine only the results you obtain from asking yourself these questions. (Numbers below refer to sentence numbers in version A to which the topics have been applied.)

Version B

(3.) **If Dr. Alanson saw a wrong being committed, he didn't turn and look away. When** did he see this? In 1980, during his third year of teaching. **What** was this wrong? Dr. Alanson read an article by a colleague and discovered it had been plagiarized from an article written by one of Alanson's professors in college. **How** did he not turn and look away? He showed the colleague's article to the chair of his department and made a suggestion to resolve the problem. **Why** did he do this? Because he felt plagiarism was a serious crime in academia.

(4.) **Dr. Alanson worked hard at living life to the fullest. Can I offer an example?** Every minute of his day was filled with activities—in addition to two to four hours a day of classes, he also spent several hours counseling students. In the evenings and on weekends he indulged in a variety of activities: skiing, playing touch football, preparing a Japanese garden in his backyard. He was also an amateur investor; last year he earned $20,000 by carefully buying and selling selected mutual funds.

Using the information provided by careful application of the topics of invention, we may now construct a more proficient paragraph. This process may at first seem mechanical to you, but it is not simply filling in the blanks; it is a process of *discovery*. Often the result is not merely a longer, fuller paragraph, but one with insights and perceptions neither you nor the reader would have guessed when looking at the original generalizations:

Version B

1 Dr. Alanson, the professor in my Introduction to Psychology
2 class, had many outstanding qualities. He was distinguished
3 by his integrity and intensity. If Dr. Alanson saw a wrong
4 being committed, he didn't turn and look away. For example,
   in 1980 during his third year of teaching he discovered that
   a colleague's article had been plagiarized from one of
5 Alanson's professors in graduate school. Because Alanson
   felt plagiarism to be a serious crime in academia, he showed

6   the article to his department chair and suggested a resolution to the problem. Also Dr. Alanson worked hard at living intensely. Every minute of his day was filled with activities—in addition to two to four hours a day of classes, he
7   also spent several hours counseling students. In the evenings and on weekends he indulged in a variety of activities: skiing, playing touch football, preparing a Japanese garden
8   in his backyard. He was also an amateur investor; last year he earned $20,000 by carefully buying and selling selected
9   mutual funds. Dr. Alanson won my admiration because the intensity with which he approached life was backed up by a moral integrity which fractured my stereotype of a fun-loving professor.

Using Subtopic Sentences

Another useful way to think of paragraph development is through **subtopic sentences**. It is often effective to follow the unifying idea with a clarifying sentence that divides the unifying idea into two or three supporting ideas or subtopics. Then a writer takes up each subtopic in turn, offering explanation or examples. (As a bridge to the next subtopic, a clear transition is essential.) As a writer, you select a key word in your unifying idea (usually an abstract, evaluative word) and divide it into categories, or think of two to three concrete examples for this abstraction. For instance, examine this unifying idea:

> **Taking classes in general education has provided me with practical information and insight.**

"Practical information and insight" are abstract and clearly need definition and development. By adding a subtopic sentence, the writer could provide a direction for developing the paragraph.

1   Taking classes in general education has provided me
2   with practical information and insight. I have gained information from my German class <A>, and unexpected insight from my history <B> and anthropology classes <C>.

Notice how the subtopics A, B, and C provide a direction for the paragraph to develop, and suggest to the writer details that make the unifying idea clearer as well as far more substantial:

1   Taking classes in general education has provided me with
2   practical information and insight. I have gained informa-
     tion from my German class <A>, and unexpected insight
3   from my history <B> and anthropology classes <C>. My
     German classes provided me with an ability to speak the
     language so that I can visit Germany and appreciate the
4   German people and German culture <A>. In my modern
     American history class I came to understand the origins of
     the Vietnam War for the first time and to appreciate my
     father's response as well as my brother's combat experience
5   <B>. In addition, I learned a great deal about the women's
     suffrage movement and now have a clear understanding of
     both the advantages and disadvantages American society
6   affords women <B>. Finally, my anthropology class did not
     simply give me insight into the culture of the Olivaro
     Indians, but I also noted how their culture differed from
7   American culture <C>. Though the Olivaros were a primi-
     tive group where the older men hunted and the women
     tended to gardens and cooked, they were also quite spiritual
8   <C>. On the other hand, Americans could buy food in
     stores— their women were not chained to the home; yet I
     found myself dismayed over our lack of a fundamental
9   spirituality <C>. Thus the information about German cul-
     ture from one class has made traveling a much more
     fulfilling experience, and the insight into American culture
     from other classes has made me a more thoughtful citizen
     and voter.

Note how each subtopic becomes expanded into a portion of the
paragraph and provides a clear guide for the reader, as well as a hint
to the writer on how to develop the paragraph.

EXERCISE 4-1

1. Identify the unifying ideas in the following paragraphs and point out the
   concrete details which the writer uses to develop them:

   (a) This tribe of Indians is isolated from the outside world. They live near
   Benares, a small town of 500 which cannot be reached by airplane,
   automobile, or train. To get to Benares, you must spend 15 days on
   a dangerous river. There are no telephones in Benares, and the mail

arrives once a week. But to get to the Undingi, you must leave Benares and climb a low mountain, then trek through the rain forest.

(b)   My good friend Jake was an unfortunate victim of the law which requires high school students to maintain at least a C− in all courses in order to pursue extracurricular activities. Going into our senior year, Jake had achieved a 3.8 grade point average. He wasn't planning to play college football, but he was an excellent center for high school ball. Regrettably Jake was unaware of the state's "C minus" law. Since he had such good grades in the past, Jake thought he didn't have to take his courses so seriously during the senior football season. Jake received a D in creative writing midway through the season and was academically disqualified from playing. While the rest of the team and I won the section championships in the Oakland Coliseum, Jake watched from the stands. To this day Jake expresses remorse over missing his last season and feels he was treated unfairly by the C− law.

(Hint: one good way of testing for details and seeing if a paragraph is sufficiently developed is to ask yourself a series of questions immediately after you have read it. For example, after you have read paragraph (b), ask yourself the following questions:

- **Who** is the athlete?

- **What** is his problem?

- **When** did it occur?

- **Where** did it occur?

- **Why** did it occur?

- **What's** the point (what is the unifying idea)? What does the athlete's situation demonstrate? What is the author's attitude about it?

2. Identify the unifying idea in the following paragraph; identify the subtopics and point out the sentences which take up those topics later in the paragraph:

       Classes that I've taken over the past 3 years in sociology, geology and psychology have given me new ways of looking at the environment around me. As a small-town country girl in a farming family, before coming to the University of North Carolina my world view was rather limited. Before taking sociology, I never stopped to consider my family as a sociological unit in which each person plays a specific role. Before geology, I never thought for a moment of the soil composition on my family farm. And before psychology I never really considered why my mother allowed long silences to enter conversations and why my father increased his drinking on certain weekends.

3. The following paragraphs show only minimal development. Expand them, using topics of invention or subtopics:

   (a)   Salaries for men and women in the medical profession are inequitable. True, doctors have more education than nurses—but not that much more. But salaries for doctors are much higher. And working conditions for nurses are quite poor.

   (b)   One point of view on abortion is adopted by the pro-choice faction. They think abortion is acceptable and legal. They think the decision should be the woman's choice.

   (c)   A word-processing program has several advantages over a typewriter. It is faster, more convenient, and cheaper.

SUMMARY

1. A proficient paragraph needs a unifying idea and should develop that idea in four to ten sentences.
2. A proficient unifying idea not only introduces a subject; it also offers a judgment, generalization, or opinion. Yet a unifying idea should not be overgeneral or too broad.
3. A proficient unifying idea should be developed with adequate support. Often concrete examples are sufficient. Many writers find topics of invention or subtopic sentences effective tools for development.

5

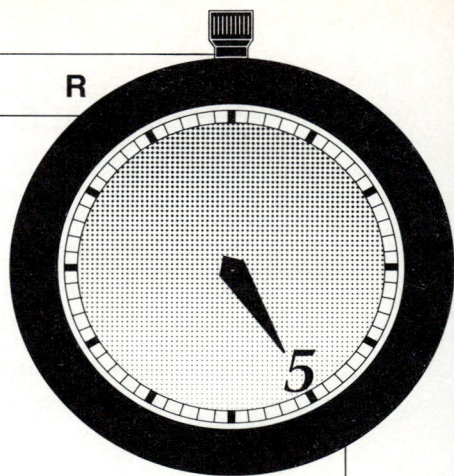

Planning Your Essay: Thesis and Introduction

IBC: INTRODUCTION, BODY, CONCLUSION
THESIS
OTHER ELEMENTS OF INTRODUCTIONS
  Hooks
  Road Map

Now that you have reviewed how to construct a proficient paragraph using the principle of unity, it is time to examine the planning of the entire essay. In some ways, an essay is much like an elongated paragraph. The essay consists of a variety of ideas—generalizations, details, responses. After brainstorming, you may have already been able to develop several paragraphs that might usefully answer the question you have been asked to write about. But you still need a Plan for the essay. You need a sense of what the whole essay will look like in order to develop parts of it effectively. A good plan often depends on a time-tested, preconceived essay structure.

IBC: INTRODUCTION, BODY, CONCLUSION

A proficient essay begins with an Introductory paragraph, develops its idea in several Body paragraphs, and comes to a clear end in a Concluding paragraph. You can remember this typical essay structure with the abbreviation **IBC**. One of the reasons this structure is effective is that readers are accustomed to it, just as they are accustomed to your designating a sentence by beginning with a capital letter and concluding with a period, or just as they are accustomed to your designating the series of related ideas that form a paragraph by beginning with an indentation.

Of course there is a logic to this structure as well, similar to the logic of the paragraph. It is effective to lead the reader into your topic with an introduction which stimulates interest, announces your subject and your particular point of view (a unifying idea for the whole essay, also known as a **thesis**), and offers a sense of direction. The **body** paragraphs offer support and explanation for that thesis. These paragraphs are called body paragraphs because they are like a human or animal body—they flesh out the skeleton the thesis provides. They offer solid substance for an abstract idea. These paragraphs offer explanation, evidence or details that are far more specific than the thesis. The **conclusion** draws matters to a close, often offering a summary or prediction (Chapter 17 discusses techniques for conclusions) and restating the **thesis.**

A typical essay formed using the IBC structure would look like this:

Paragraph 1. Introduction
Paragraph 2. Develops topic A ⎤
Paragraph 3. Develops topic B ⎪ BODY
Paragraph 4. Develops topic C ⎬ PARAGRAPHS
Paragraph 5. Develops topic D ⎦
Paragraph 6. Conclusion

This particular structure would generate six paragraphs. Many of you may be familiar with the five-paragraph essay, which uses a similar structure, but develops only three main ideas in its body paragraphs. These paragraphs may use various strategies of development (narrative, comparison, process: see Chapter 6), but essentially they support or extend the **thesis** in the introductory paragraph. The important point is not to tie yourself to a rigid structure, to feel you must have a certain specified number of paragraphs. Rather, you should concentrate on how each part of the

IBC structure functions in relation to the whole. You especially need to see how an effective introduction can itself provide a useful plan for the essay.

THESIS

The core of an introduction is a proficient thesis that will unify your essay. With such a thesis, you *clearly* respond to the exam question or the demand made of you, you sufficiently *narrow* the topic so that you can develop it in the time allotted, and you provide some *direction* for a reader—some indication of where your essay will lead and how it will develop its unifying idea. A good thesis *doesn't* just echo the question and promise to write an essay about it; a good thesis states specifics and suggests analysis and judgment. An effective thesis does not merely restate the obvious or offer a platitude. A working thesis is a kind of **contract** with the reader. In it you assert a view or attitude which the reader can expect you to explain and support in your essay. We know that a contract must be sufficiently specific to offer anything to either of the parties that sign it. Similarly, a proficient thesis must be sufficiently narrow to offer interest to a reader and clear direction for a writer. We also know that a contract raises expectations of performance and allows either party to back out if expectations are not met. Likewise, if your essay fails to meet the expectations aroused by the thesis, your reader may back out—and stop reading. If you don't live up to your contract because the thesis statement is weak or poorly constructed, your essay will probably be seen as nonproficient.

The best way to judge how a thesis works is to look at possible theses for some sample questions:

Q1: Analyze the characteristics and qualities of a good instructor. Use specific examples—either positive or negative—to support your points.

Q2: Write an essay in which you argue for or against the present way we determine salaries for particular kinds of work.

Suppose you came up with a test thesis like this for Question 1: "A good instructor has various qualities and characteristics. I will develop them in the following essay." Though this responds to the question, it offers **no** direction for your essay. A reader would have no idea from this thesis what you considered to be the essential qualities of a good instructor. He would have no idea what he might find in your essay. Why? Because this kind of thesis suffers from two defects: it has not narrowed[1] the topic, and it is full of **essayese**—talking about writing the essay, promising that it will do something, but not specifically saying what it will do. Essayese is typified by statements like **"In the following essay I will discuss several points"; "I will write about the various characteristics . . . and will conclude by . . . ."** Essayese is wasteful and misleading. It is a weak method to begin an essay because it says virtually nothing. Avoid it if you want to write proficiently. Echo key words from the question, but don't simply copy the question or rearrange its words into a statement. **You must add something specific (observation, opinion, judgment) of your own to create a workable thesis and avoid essayese.**

Instead of essayese, write a thesis that narrows your topic and promises the reader relevant information and justification for specific judgments: "A good instructor may be rare, but typically displays an engaging manner <1>, an ability to organize material clearly <2>, and fairness in dealing with diverse student needs <3>." You need not agree that these are the characteristics of a good instructor, but this thesis offers a clear direction for the essay to take. The writer has sufficiently narrowed the characteristics of a good teacher from an almost infinite number to three; he has not wasted a reader's time with essayese. In order to create this list, the writer has *judged* the characteristics of a good instructor, and he has specifically stated those judgments.

Let's examine a test thesis for Question 2: "Money is a problem for many people." This thesis gets the writer off to a poor start. It does not clearly focus on the question and instead offers a platitude, a statement so broad and obvious that virtually all readers will acknowledge it, but very few readers will consider it of any interest. You might notice that this test thesis is also weak because it doesn't mention any of the key words: **salaries, determine** or **work.** An introduction (and an essay) that begins with this thesis statement

---

[1] To **narrow** a thesis means to address the question sufficiently to provide a coherent, meaningful answer in the time allotted. As we have already suggested, a thesis is a unifying idea, much like that for a body paragraph. But the thesis differs from the unifying idea of a body paragraph because a thesis is broader—it is broad enough to include the unifying ideas of paragraphs. There is no absolute here, but clearly the kind of idea governing a book of 300 pages differs from that which governs a 30-page article, which in turn differs from that which governs a 5-page essay exam. Just as a unifying idea offers direction for a paragraph, so a properly narrowed thesis implies a workable **plan** for your essay.

might be about the problems of budgeting, figuring income tax, adjusting allowances for children, or paying for a college education. And if you allow this to remain as your thesis statement, you might get temporarily sidetracked onto one of those issues and fail to address the question directly.

A revised thesis that focuses on the issue of salaries might be: "Salaries in the United States have been unfair over the last half century. Instead of letting the market and politics determine salaries, we should guarantee workers a wage based on the years of education required for their work <1> and the amount of responsibility for other human beings demanded by their work <2>." Such a thesis clearly responds to the question (it disagrees with the current method of establishing salaries) and offers a direction for developing the essay. The thesis also narrows the topic by listing two criteria for setting salaries; these criteria can be developed in the following body paragraphs. [Note that this particular thesis consists of two sentences.]

So, how do you determine if you have a proficient thesis? Have you echoed **key words** from the question? This will keep you from losing focus, or writing off the topic. Have you avoided **essayese?** If you have, you state your specific ideas on the topic, you avoid wasting the reader's time, and you avoid pretending you have an idea and plan for your essay when you don't. Have you narrowed the topic? If you have, you offer personal experience, judgments, or particular examples that indicate the direction of your essay.

EXERCISE 5-1

Evaluate the following questions and test thesis statements. Use these criteria: Does the thesis echo key words? Is it free of essayese? Does it narrow the topic? Does it provide a clear direction for the reader?

Q3: Analyze a procedure which you believe is inefficient and discuss what you think could be done to make it more efficient.

   A. "The world is full of inefficient procedures."

   B. "Registering for college courses every fall is inefficient, and could be improved if every student were first required to see a counselor."

Q4. What makes a good leader?

   A. "The qualities of a good leader are the subject of this essay. In the first paragraph I will analyze what those qualities are. I will then give examples of leaders I knew who had those qualities. Finally I will conclude by explaining how qualities like these lead to success."

B. "Good leaders can be found in colleges, corporations, and countries; but all share several outstanding qualities — self-confidence, vision, intelligence, and sympathy with others different from themselves."

Once you have a thesis, check as you write your essay to see if you keep focusing on this thesis, if you adhere to the contract you have made with the reader. About once a paragraph as you compose your draft, make sure you are still on track. To check, see if unifying ideas of body paragraphs echo key words from the thesis.

Your test thesis need not be perfect; do not be afraid to alter it slightly as you write. Often you will find that your concluding paragraph includes a restatement of your thesis that contains less essayese, is narrower, and better fits the direction your essay has taken than the actual thesis in your introductory paragraph. Why? Because now that you have finished your essay, these elements are all clearer to you. If this is the case, replace the thesis in your introductory paragraph with the superior thesis from the final paragraph — then revise the final paragraph. In your draft, it might help you to underline your thesis so that you can identify it quickly for reference. In the rest of this chapter, we have underlined thesis statements in introductory paragraphs to make them easier for you to locate and examine.

OTHER ELEMENTS OF INTRODUCTIONS

An introductory paragraph states your thesis, and you now know the criteria for a proficient thesis. But what else should a proficient introduction contain? Remember that one rule of thumb (from Chapter 2) warns against one-sentence paragraphs, and this rule remains emphatically true for the first paragraph of your essay. Baldly stating your thesis in a one-sentence paragraph, no matter how carefully worded it may be, is rarely proficient and often antagonizes readers. You also need a technique to involve the reader immediately: a **hook** or attention-getter. You may also need a **road map** to the topics of body paragraphs to guide the reader, and to guide you as you construct your essay.

Though you often compose a test thesis **first** in writing your essay, the thesis is rarely the first sentence of your introduction. In fact, your introductory paragraph will generally have the following structure:

Hook

Thesis

Road Map

Hooks

A hook or attention-getter is a device (several sentences) that intrigues the reader before you introduce your thesis and develop your support. You might think hooks are unimportant in timed writing.[2] Since the primary purpose of a hook is to snare a reader, many students feel that the entertainment value of an intriguing opening is unnecessary in writing which a reader **must** read. We know that professors have to read our exams, that paid readers must read proficiency exams, that someone is paid to read law boards and the CPA exam, that colleagues at work ought to read our memos, that addressees should read reports especially designed for them. These audiences do not at first seem like the casual readers who glance through a magazine, newspaper, or bookshelf looking for something to catch their interest. Still, even though they must read and they are often paid to do so, readers at work and at school will appreciate and respond to writing that makes an effort to intrigue them. Often a good hook will wake up a nodding reader, or reinvigorate eyes for which reading has become a mindless, mechanical process. More significantly, a good hook is one of the author's signals to a reader that the reader is in capable hands—that the author is proficient.

A hook is one of the signs of a proficient writer—someone who can turn virtually any material or subject into reading matter with verve and interest. For some obvious chronological and psychological reasons, the beginning is a crucial place for interesting the reader. This is why movies often begin with especially noteworthy sequences, why after-dinner speakers often begin with jokes, and

---

[2]Though hooks are important, you may wish to reserve the time to write them until the end of your period—and initially pay more attention in the introductory paragraph to thesis and road map. Though we discuss "hooks" in this chapter dealing with introductions, you will probably find that many of these techniques can be used effectively at any point in an essay.

why the writers of great epics and novels began provocatively or powerfully. Here are some arresting first lines: "Call me Ishmael"[3]; "If you really want to hear about it, the first thing you'll probably want to know is where I was born . . . and all that David Copperfield kind of crap"[4]; "This is the story of a man, one who was never at a loss"[5] ; "April is the cruellest month."[6] These writers are trying to create a puzzle, to intrigue the reader, to give their addition to the word-heap some style, originality, or significance.[7] You need not begin your essay with such memorable hooks as these, but there are a number of useful techniques which will earn your writing the attention it deserves: **question, anecdote, analogy, quotation or dialogue, description,** and **provocative assertion.** (These examples don't exhaust the possibilities, but most of them can prove effective when you are under time pressure.)

Question

Because you have only a limited amount of time to construct a hook, using a question may be the most effective way. Virtually any statement or approach can be made more appealing by turning it into a question. The sense of mystery and suspense and the sense that the reader is participating are both involved in the appeal of the question. Asking several questions in succession is also effective. Note how the following introductory paragraph uses the question technique in responding to Question 1 (see Q1, page 68).[8]

> Have you ever encountered an instructor you really appreciated? Have you wondered why that teacher was so

---

[3]Herman Melville, *Moby-Dick*.

[4]J.D. Salinger, *The Catcher in the Rye*.

[5]Homer, *The Odyssey*.

[6]T.S. Eliot, *The Waste Land*.

[7]Often the writing at the beginning of a great work is notably more powerful, more controlled, more elegant, and suggests the writer took more time in crafting it. But this writing is not necessarily what the novelist or poet **first** wrote. Often your idea for a hook may come to you after most of your essay is complete. That is okay. Just put it in the appropriate place in the introductory paragraph.

[8]Be careful in constructing introductory questions to make sure that probable answers lead the reader toward your topic, rather than on a wild goose chase away from it. Provocative questions can gain a reader's interest, but the reader will soon lose interest if there is a feeling the questions are unguided or merely a device.

effective? What was it about her? Was it simply her knowledge of the subject matter? Obviously, the qualities that make a good instructor are often subtle, not apparent at first. But four qualities are critical: knowledge of the subject, ability to organize material, fairness in responding to diverse student needs, and a sense of humor.

[Note how these questions set up the list of criteria the author will develop in the thesis.]

Anecdote

Even though your thesis is by nature abstract or general, a good way to hook a reader is by making the subject concrete from the very beginning. Begin with an anecdote (a short, revealing—often humorous—narrative) that bears on the topic. Be sure that the story can be effectively told within the scope of a paragraph:

> Zoom! An eraser whizzed past me. Mr. Storm was at it again—he would throw blackboard erasers during lulls in the class, or at students who seemed to doze or be preoccupied with subjects other than English. It was one of his many idiosyncracies—along with his white hair, the fact that he was still teaching at 80, and the "rules" for writing posted in large black script on sheets hung from the blackboard. By the way, when he threw, he always missed—since he wanted his students to survive and digest the material he presented. One of my most memorable teachers from junior high, he demonstrated some of the characteristics of a good instructor—a certain amount of healthy terror, verve, organization, and a sense of humor.

[Notice how the anecdote consists of concrete details, creating some suspense as to the results of the thrown eraser, but also illustrating most of the characteristics of the good instructor listed in the thesis. Also notice how the introduction ends with a clearly stated thesis which signals the end of the story and the beginning of the essay.]

Analogy

Because of their unpredictability, analogies often intrigue readers and are thus effective ways to generate introductory paragraphs. An analogy compares your subject to something unrelated, but usually quite common, in order to reveal unperceived aspects of your subject. You can generate an analogy by beginning a sentence with your subject, then adding the phrase "is like" and completing the sentence. Often analogies draw out the comparison for nearly a whole paragraph (see Q2, page 68).

A nation's economy or market system is like an automobile. Every little part is essential to smooth, overall functioning. Remove a tire, and the car will jerk along the road at greatly reduced speed. Drop the windshield wipers, and it's dangerous in the rain. Get rid of the seats to save money, and no one can find a comfortable position from which to steer. Tinkering with long-established economic structures has the same results. Our nation's salary structure has been built up over long decades of decisions, confrontations, laws and adjustments. It may be unfair, but tinkering with it now could easily lead to disaster, just like eliminating the seats from an automobile because they cost too much to make.

[Note: While readers are familiar with automobiles, they may have difficulty understanding the vast system of a nation's economy, or difficulty seeing beyond their own desire for a salary increase. The automobile analogy makes the economy understandable and the judgment offered believable.]

Quotation or Dialogue

Famous quotations from renowned authorities typically engage a reader's interest and can give your ideas background and prestige from the start. But during an exam, it is often difficult to remember an appropriate line from Shakespeare, the Bible, a famous economist, scientist, or educator. Instead, remembered or created dialogues can effectively introduce issues, particularly on argumentative topics. With dialogue a writer can benefit from the techniques of fiction, including using colloquial language and spouting outrageous opinions for which the writer is not called to account, while still offering information and introducing a serious topic.

"I can't believe it! My parents and I spent over $20,000 on my college education; the professors have ground me into the dirt; I've worked 40 hours a week for 5 years; and the most I can expect is a measly $16,000 a year for a starting salary."

"Joe, that's nothing. My father has worked as a lawyer for the state for twenty years now. He has to visit murderers in prison and defend them in court, and do you think they're grateful? No! And what kind of salary can he make? About one-third of what he'd get if he went into private practice in personal injury law. It's just not fair!"

These opinions are typical of the conflicts arising over the justice of salaries in various lines of work. Hours of preparation, years of education and sacrifice—none of these are consistently taken into account by our current system of setting wages. <u>We need a more rational salary system—one based directly on educational preparation and effort.</u>

[Note how dialogue relates directly to the thesis, offering opposing views and suggesting the need for a salary structure that will satisfy diverse individuals and occupations. Technically the dialogue creates a three-paragraph introduction; remember that it is not always necessary to confine introductory material to one paragraph.]

Description

The trouble with most introductions that lack hooks is that they are general, vague, or bland. Often nonproficient writers fill paragraphs with a series of empty abstractions. To counter this tendency, you can begin your introductory paragraph with descriptive details (aspects that can be interpreted with one or more of the five senses) which illustrate or epitomize your thesis. Vivid details like these typically appear in body paragraphs, but they can be appropriate as a representative illustration which will be expanded later in the essay:

> Laura is a typical nurse. And her workday is typically hectic. In the emergency room she is ordered around by doctors, yelled at by patients' relatives, and assaulted by the odors of urine or of patients who haven't bathed for weeks. She must draw blood from 20 patients, some of whom are intravenous drug users with telltale pinpricks on their arms—any of these patients may suffer from AIDS. The walls of the rooms she works in are a vomitous lime green, and the smell of disinfectant permeates her day. The doctors who occasionally work alongside her earn four times her pay. Is this fair? No! <u>As a nation we need to adjust our salary scales so doctors and nurses have pay that is not so disparate.</u>

[Note how vivid details set the scene for the thesis and make it provisionally credible, earning sympathy for its position before the writer even begins the argument.]

Provocative Assertion

The job of the hook is to grab the reader's attention. Occasionally the best way to do this lies in the nature of the thesis itself. A thesis that makes a provocative assertion intrigues readers simply because it is not a run-of-the-mill approach, because it challenges their established ways of thinking. To create such a thesis, begin by stating the "obvious" idea with which "everyone" agrees—then contradict it:

> Workers are paid based on what they are worth, on their hours of preparation, on how the "market" values their job, on their years of education—in other words, salaries are based on some rational system. Right? No, wrong! There is no rational basis for any system of salaries. A talented observer can always detect numerous inequities, arbitrary pay scales, illegal wage systems. A professional basketball player earns millions of dollars per year, far more than a doctor. Yet a doctor has spent 10 years more in education and preparation before he can earn a salary and earns far less. An executive for a Japanese corporation earns a fraction of an American executive's pay. Yet Japanese corporations currently outperform American corporations in profits, sales, efficiency, and product quality. Surprisingly, the manager of a certain municipal utility in California earns more than the President of the United States. <u>In short, there is just no rhyme or reason to salaries—to compare salaries in hopes of achieving equity or sense is a fruitless task.</u>

[Note how the writer begins by destroying a variety of accepted opinions in order to suggest that all salary systems must be and are irrational. Part of the force of this hook also comes from astute use of concrete detail.]

You can use any of these hooks or perhaps invent one of your own. But it is not an effective technique to always use the same type of hook. It might work once—on a single exam—but in any situation where you are likely to encounter the same readers repeatedly, using the same hook over and over can become mechanical both for you and for them. A proficient writer commands a *variety* of strategies and does not rely on only one approach.

EXERCISE 5-2

In response to the following topics, write three introductory paragraphs, using a different type of hook (question, anecdote, analogy, quotation or dialogue, description, or provocative assertion in each). Underline your thesis statement.

1. Write an essay in which you examine television as a positive or negative influence on American life.
2. Analyze the value of your academic major as a preparation for a career.
3. Discuss a serious problem faced by modern society.

Road Map

After engaging the reader's attention with a hook, and stating clearly your idea in the thesis, you should also add a **road map** to your introduction. A road map guides the reader through the thicket of words in your essay. It points out the main paths so the reader does not get lost. Though not required for every introduction, a road map can quickly reveal the structure and strategy of your essay—both for yourself and the reader. Just as your thesis functions as a contract with the reader, so your road map functions as a kind of table of contents. A proficient road map alerts the reader to the central organization of the essay by announcing main topics to be covered in the essay's body.

A road map is often a sentence (or several sentences) following the thesis, although sometimes it may be incorporated within the thesis itself; many proficient writers join it to the thesis with a semicolon. Typically a road map contains an element for each body paragraph. This element may be a sentence, a phrase, or even a single word—and it echoes the unifying idea in the corresponding body paragraph. In this way the road map reveals the organization of the essay—and the order in which ideas will be covered. It is very important to use the same order of ideas in your body paragraphs as in the road map: refer to the introduction's road map as you write the body of your essay, just as you refer to your thesis occasionally.[9] The following schema shows how the road map works:

Introductory paragraph: HOOK
THESIS
ROAD MAP: TOPICS A, B, C, D

---

[9]You can change the road map as you write. If you find that one element in the road map's list does not work and you cannot construct a body paragraph for it, omit it. If you find that the order in which you originally listed topics is unworkable, or you just did not follow it, alter the road map in the introductory paragraph. The proficient strategy is to provide a useful guide for the reader by making the road map consistent with the body of the essay—while avoiding essayese ("In the first paragraph I will examine . . .").

Paragraph 2: TOPIC A

Paragraph 3: TOPIC B

Paragraph 4: TOPIC C

Paragraph 5: TOPIC D

Concluding paragraph

Here is an example of an introductory paragraph with hook, thesis, and road map:

> Are students being taught to study effectively? It's easy for a teacher to throw a textbook and a syllabus in front of a student and say, "Read chapters 1, 2, and 3. Come back next Monday, and I'll lecture on them." The student is expected to go home, digest the material, and return Monday to be enlightened by the professor. There is a mid-term exam, and then a final at the end of the course, and on these the student is expected to regurgitate the material. The typical professor never offers the student advice on study habits. This pattern is exactly what I have observed in my fellow students for the past four years: these students get assignments, digest them and regurgitate them. But then, just as quickly, students forget what they have learned. If teachers were to introduce study techniques to their classes, students would learn efficiently and retain the information. Teachers could explain how to create a record and study sheet by careful note-taking <A>, could suggest occasionally reading similar material in other texts and professional journals to reinforce the information <B>, and could provide review sessions in which they encourage students to imagine challenging exam questions <C>.

Notice that this paragraph begins with a hook combining question, dialogue and anecdotal material, before it announces the thesis and provides a road map. Given this road map, we would expect a body paragraph structure such as the following:

Paragraph 2: <A> Note-taking

Paragraph 3: <B> Parallel reading

Paragraph 4: <C> Exam-question imagining

As the road map is part of your contract with the reader, it would be incorrect to list, for example, "careful note-taking" if you had no intention of developing note-taking in the body of your essay. Similarly, it would be confusing to take up exam-question imagining in Paragraph 2 or parallel reading in Paragraph 4—given the order they were originally listed in the road map.

What *have* you contracted to do by writing this thesis and road map? You have agreed to provide your reader with certain specific information. For example, according to the contract, Paragraph 4 would explain what imagining exam questions is like and offer instances of how it might be used, in, say, a sociology class. Given the thesis, this paragraph would also have to explain how exam-question imagining is superior to the "digest-regurgitate" method. Also, it should explain why imagining the questions in a study session and in the weeks before the exam is better than simply trying to memorize the text the night before. Given this analysis, a good unifying idea for paragraph 4 might be: "In addition to explaining note-taking and parallel reading, instructors could describe the study technique of imagining exam questions. This would help the students not only to take the final exam for that particular course, but also would force them into an imaginative confrontation with the subject matter of other courses—and comprehension of that subject matter would be likely to endure." Note how key words—**instructors, study technique, imagining exam questions**—keep both writer and reader focused on the topic and fulfill the contract made by the thesis and road-map.

EXERCISE 5-3

Develop a road map sentence for each of the following thesis statements. Indicate what would be the topics for body paragraphs; then write a unifying idea for each body paragraph based on your road map.

1. The dating process has several phases.
2. Hospital emergency rooms are inefficient.
3. My education began as a rote process and ended by drawing out my potential.

EXERCISE 5-4

Develop proficient introductory paragraphs for the following questions. Put brackets around the material you consider your hook, underline your thesis, and circle your road map.

1. Examine a critical incident in your life and explain why its effects have been so long-lasting.
2. Should national television networks be forbidden from forecasting election results before all polls are closed?

SUMMARY

1. A proficient essay includes the thesis in an introductory paragraph, and uses an IBC (Introduction-Body-Conclusion) structure.
2. The key to a proficient essay is a proficient thesis, which echoes key words from the exam question, has narrowed the topic sufficiently, avoids essayese, and provides direction for the reader.
3. A proficient introductory paragraph begins with a hook which might be any of the following: question, anecdote, description, quotation or dialogue, analogy, or provocative assertion.
4. A proficient introductory paragraph offers an indication of the topics and order for body paragraphs by providing a road map.

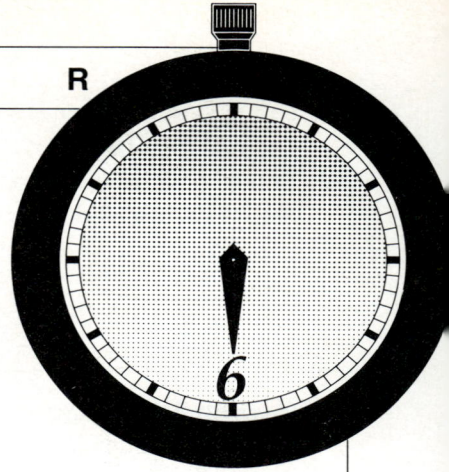

Developing Body Paragraphs and Ordering Your Essay

SAMPLE EXAM
USING MODES TO DEVELOP PARAGRAPHS
  Narration
  Other Modes of Development
PROVIDING TRANSITIONS
  Transitions Within Paragraphs
  Transitions Between Paragraphs

SAMPLE EXAM

The Issue: It is often said that we never stop learning until our dying day and that we learn infinitely more and infinitely better in the "classroom of life" than we can ever hope to learn in the classrooms of our schools and universities. Other wisdom, however, suggests that schooling provides a far more satisfying and balanced education.

The Essay Question: Drawing on your own experiences, readings, or observations, write an essay that discusses the relationship between life learning and formal education learning. Indicate which you feel is more valuable and explain why.

The Essay:

A Visit to the Castle of Chillon

1   Life is full of many experiences. My life has been full too. One in particular stands out, and I regard it as a learning experience of the first order.

2   When I was 19 I took my first European trip. I remember it especially because I was still young enough to get a cheap, second class Eurailpass. You should have seen the hassle my parents had getting that from the travel agent. At any rate they, my brother Gunner, and I all got on a plane in New York and landed 6 hours later in Paris.

3   Within a week we were in Switzerland and that's where my experience begins. Switzerland is known for its watches, its chocolate, its Swiss army knives, and the Swiss Alps. But while my parents did some shopping and took us to Montreux for the jazz festival, I was bored until I met Antoinette. She had been to Europe before, knew how to order in French and German, knew all the best cafes in Montreux, and also some of the popular hangouts. Then the trip began to become really fun for me.

4   Toni and I would sit in a cafe in Montreux discussing poetry and planning our tour for the day. One day we would go to Lausanne for shopping. The next we would take a boat across the Lake to France. Lake Geneva, or Lake Leman as it is sometimes called, is one of the largest lakes in Europe and is bordered by three countries.

5   One day as Toni and I were talking and drinking a German beer—Spaten from Munich—she mentioned that Lord Byron had written a poem connected with a little peninsula and castle not too distant from our cafe: the castle of Chillon. At first it didn't sound very intriguing to me. I was far more interested in his poem Don Juan; besides I hadn't come to Europe to spend my days in dusty museums.

6   Nevertheless, we were bored that day so we hired a taxi and went to Chillon. I couldn't believe how much I would

learn there and how classroom experience would pale by comparison.

7   I remember entering by the gate. I noticed how isolated the Castle was and how it would function effectively during a siege. It seemed built out of rock from the Lake, and it was solid, massive, foreboding. I even remember that the tickets cost 2 Swiss francs, about the cost of another Spaten beer.

8   The castle had many rooms and floors and we had entered on the ground floor. Each floor held a new experience. I remember one room in particular. On its walls hung torture devices, various collars and thumbscrews and other works of metal with which human beings tried to gain from other human beings morsels of information that would later be crucial to history. I wondered how many people had once bled in that room. Toni took a picture of me with my wrists encased in one of these devices.

9   On another floor there were little crevices and narrow windows through which you could easily see the lake or shoot arrows and pour boiling oil on attackers or unwanted visitors. I remember standing at the side of one of these openings and looking out on the lake. Today it was spectacular: sunny, cool, and inviting. Years ago it must have seemed foreboding.

10   One room had served as a prison. On a pillar you could find where Lord Byron carved his name. The man who had written The Prisoner of Chillon and Don Juan. This was certainly more impressive than a class in English literature.

11   There was no access to the roof. But when I was on the top floor, I imagined standing on that roof just inches above my head and repelling invaders from France or Germany. This experience was etched in my memory deeper than any history textbook page.

12   As I walked through the castle I noticed that the bathrooms were nowhere to be found in the building, and thought how difficult life must have been in those days compared to today with the convenience of indoor plumbing. True, the bedrooms were gigantic compared to my dinky room at home. But I imagined heating the place must have been a continual struggle in winter. Maybe this is why we have abandoned castles and preferred the ranchstyle home and a summer vacation.

13   When we left I bought a guidebook explaining the history of Chillon and even mentioning the Byron poem. But I never took a college class on European history. Wasn't the direct experience of the castle enough in itself? Not to mention less boring.

What score would you give this essay and why? (You may want to re-read the scoring guidelines in chapter 1 to help you decide.) Has this writer appropriately addressed the exam question? What problems, if any, do you have with his essay? Please take a few minutes to write down your responses to "Castle of Chillon" before you continue reading this chapter.

You should have given the "Castle of Chillon" essay a "3" or failing score. Though it has many strengths, the essay fails primarily because it uses narration (particularly *unreflective narration*) as the only method of developing a response to the exam question. The following discussion explains the disadvantages of using unreflective narrative and shows you more proficient techniques for developing an essay.

USING MODES TO DEVELOP PARAGRAPHS

Students often falter on essay exams when an exam question invites narration; their essays can turn into long, overly detailed stories which stray from the thesis and do not appropriately address the essay question. Stories told orally can be amusing. Written stories, though easy to compose, can be hard for a reader—because often the point of the story or value of a particular event is not apparent until the end, and the reader must plod through seemingly pointless detail to get there. Thus, narratives often lack proficiency because they include excessive detail, lose focus, and ignore or avoid analysis—they do not *explain why* the events happened as they did. These flaws are common to *unreflective narrative*. However, *reflective narrative*, or carefully selected narrative details that make an important point or support a main idea, can be an effective strategy for developing an essay.

Narration is one way to present information in an essay. But often exam questions may require other methods of developing body paragraphs. Some exam questions suggest—or even require—this development in a certain mode. A **mode** is a general format or plan for arranging details in a paragraph (or sometimes in an entire essay). Common modes are narration, comparison, process analysis, and cause/effect. Although an entire essay can be developed in a given mode, more often, and especially on proficiency exams, students may have to develop various aspects of a thesis by employing different modes. For example, they may have to **narrate** an incident, then **analyze what caused** the incident. Or they may be asked to **describe** an unjust law, then **compare** it with alternatives. Or they may be asked to **argue** against salaries for certain professions and may find that the best way to develop this argument would be to use **comparison.** Therefore, understanding how to develop body paragraphs in these modes is an important strategy in achieving proficiency.

Finally, transition is important to essay continuity; proficient writers know how to use transitions to keep readers on track and to keep the focus on the essay's unifying ideas. Proficient use of transitions shows the reader why sentences and paragraphs are arranged in a particular order and how the ideas in paragraphs relate to the thesis. Weak or non-existent transitions make it difficult for a reader to see the relationships between the ideas presented in the essay.

Narration

The mode which the writer of "Castle of Chillon" used to develop his essay is **narration.** Narration involves relating a story or describing a situation so a reader can understand the facts and details of the event. Narration can be used to establish the circumstances that will be the basis for analysis in an essay. In fact, many exams require a paragraph or two of narration to "set the scene" for an essay: you may be asked to describe a situation in which you had to make a compromise, relate an incident that tested your character, tell about a time when you needed to be alone, or describe an admirable leader or teacher. You may also use narration in giving examples to support your points; for example, you may tell the story of your first day in class to support your claim that your English teacher strived to establish rapport with students.

Problems with Narration

Though narration is a way to present pertinent information in an essay, it is not an effective way to develop an *entire* essay. Narration does not require much, if any, analysis, but an *essay* does require analysis; an essay is more than just a story. In an essay, you don't want to just tell what happened; you also want to **analyze** causes of the events, effects of the events, what you learned from the situations, why people acted as they did. Furthermore, in an essay, details are organized by *main points* (stated as the unifying ideas of paragraphs), while in a story, details are organized by time or sequence.

The "Castle of Chillon" essay fails primarily because it is developed solely through narration. The writer has mistaken a story for an essay. He simply relates the details—and some are quite trivial—of his trip to Europe and his tour of the castle, and leaves the analysis up to the reader—"Wasn't the direct experience of the castle enough in itself?"

But, you might say, the "Castle of Chillon" essay is well-organized. The writer carefully follows a time sequence which makes the essay easy to follow. The paragraphs also seem unified—each paragraph deals with one aspect of his trip. And there is a continuity—the temporal sequence establishes a transition from one event to the next. Aren't these qualities of a proficient essay? One of the dangers of developing an essay through narration is that what you are writing *appears* to have appropriate structure when it really does not. For example, though the essay follows an orderly time sequence, there is no clearly stated thesis and road map in the introduction. What point is the writer making? How does the story respond to the exam question?

Even though his essay *suggests* that the writer prefers life learning to classroom learning, he never makes his thesis clear. A reader absorbs many details of the writer's trip without any clear guidance as to how they relate to a thesis. Also, though each paragraph of "Castle of Chillon" deals with a separate aspect of the trip, few paragraphs have a **unifying idea,** or a statement that identifies the subject of the paragraph and expresses an opinion, generalization or judgment (see Chapter 4 for more information on unifying ideas). For example, in paragraphs 7, 8, 9, 10, 11, and 12—which describe the castle tour—the "unifying ideas" are simply statements of fact used to establish the area of the castle the writer is describing:

"I remember entering by the gate."

"The castle had many rooms and floors and we had entered on the ground floor."

"On another floor there were little crevices and narrow windows. . . ."

"There was no access to the roof."

Furthermore, when you develop an essay through narration, it is easy to stray from the exam question because you are concentrating too much on detail and not enough on analysis. For example, "Castle of Chillon" is laden with trivial, unnecessary detail that goes nowhere. What is the writer's point in paragraph 3, for example, in mentioning that "Switzerland is known for its watches, its chocolate, its Swiss Army knives, and the Swiss Alps"? (He doesn't explain this detail, but in fact it does relate to trade and tourism.) Why does he mention, in paragraph 4, that "Lake Geneva . . . is one of the largest lakes in Europe and is bordered by three countries"? Is he suggesting he learned first-hand that Switzerland is a central location in Europe and is, therefore, influenced by other countries? Because the writer does not relate these details to a thesis, they seem pointless.

The writer's narrative development results in a stream-of-consciousness account of his experience: he records details as he remembers observing them, regardless of their importance. Note, for example, the seventh paragraph: "I remember entering by the gate. I noticed how isolated the castle was and how it would function effectively during a siege. It seemed to be built out of rock from the Lake, and it was solid, massive, foreboding. I even remember that the tickets cost 2 Swiss Francs, about the cost of another Spaten beer." While these details are interesting, he does not clearly relate them to the subject of classroom learning versus life learning, and the comment on the ticket cost is irrelevant in the paragraph.

The writer of "Castle of Chillon" may have thought that by simply telling the story of his trip, he could make readers understand easily that this life experience was far more valuable to him than any classroom experience. He even hints at this idea throughout his essay, for example, in paragraphs 1, 6, 10, and 11.

"One in particular stands out, and I regard it as a learning experience of the first order."

"I couldn't believe how much I would learn there and how classroom experience would pale by comparison."

"This was certainly more impressive than a class in English literature."

"This experience was etched in my memory deeper than any history textbook page."

But because his story lacks a clearly stated thesis and paragraphs with unifying ideas to develop that thesis, his point is lost. However, with extensive editing, this writer's story could be very effective in supporting an argument on the benefits of learning through life experiences.

Using Narration Effectively

Exam questions may require some narration, but how should this story-telling be handled? First, writers must be selective in the details they present. A reader does not need to know every little aspect of the situation or event. Presenting excessive, trivial detail is called "unreflective narrative"—the writer is not thinking about (or *reflecting upon*) what really *needs* to be said. For example, in "Castle of Chillon" the writer's comments about his girlfriend's ability to order in French and German or his drinking beer and discussing poetry are not at all important to his story; nor did he need to mention his brother or parents—they played no part in the story. His comments on his excursions to Montreux and Lausanne are also misleading. Instead, he should have focused his story on what a powerful learning experience touring the castle was for him. The story could have been condensed to several paragraphs at most, and in other paragraphs he could have analyzed how people learn more from practice than from theory. When using narration in an essay, writers should select *revealing details*—details that highlight the situation, so the reader gets a general understanding but is not burdened with inessential particulars. This careful selection of detail is called **reflective narrative**—reflecting on important aspects.

A second point to remember when writing narrative is that the story must be told in a specific sequence. This sequence, whether temporal (time order) or spatial (physical appearance) establishes continuity and helps readers more clearly comprehend the details. In other words, you start at the beginning, present the details in an orderly sequence, and end at the end. This may seem like common sense, but often, under time pressure, writers relate a story or describe a situation *as the details come to mind*, not as it actually happened, which can confuse readers. "Castle of Chillon," though it has many problems, does follow a temporal and spatial sequence; in fact, this careful adherence to sequence gives the essay structure. For example, in telling of the castle tour, the writer takes his readers on a spatial "tour"—he starts with the entrance gate and the ground floor, takes readers up the stairs and through the halls and ends on the highest floor. Also, he comments on the bedrooms, the prison room, and the windows in separate paragraphs. His chronological sequence of relating facts as they occurred day by day—leaving from New York and arriving in Paris, moving on to Switzerland, going to Montreux, discussing his daily activities and finally his trip to Chillon—is very logical and orderly. These sequences help readers to keep track of all the details.

EXERCISE 6-1

1. Omit unnecessary detail in the following narrative paragraph.

TOPIC: Relate an incident that led to your having to make a compromise with another person.

> My roommate was such a lazy and sloppy person, and I was at the end of my patience with her bad habits. I met her three years ago in my biology class when we were partners in a project that required us to dissect a frog, and she seemed like a really nice person and certainly looked neat and orderly. Each day when she came home, she would open the door, throw her books on the floor, walk over to the refrigerator, open it, take out a beer, open it, walk to the couch, sit down, turn on the T.V. with the remote control, and that was it for the next few hours. This was her typical routine; she didn't even do her homework or study, and her grades were really suffering. It didn't matter if there were dirty dishes piled high in the sink, if the garbage needed to be emptied, if there were papers on the dining room table or if her clothes were on the floor. Sometimes she would monopolize the phone for hours on end, often revealing embarrassing and obnoxious details of her personal life as she chatted with her boyfriend whom she had been dating for three years. When I got home, I'd open the door and walk in to this mess with this lazy "slug" sitting on the couch, drinking beer, watching T.V., talking on the phone about who knows

what, ignoring the surroundings. Sometimes she would be wearing *my* sweats which also really made me mad because she never would ask before borrowing my clothes. So I would have to start washing the dishes, or dump the garbage, or clear a week's worth of newspapers that had accumulated on the dining room table. And I really didn't like to do that because I had much better things to do such as my homework, or visiting my boyfriend or sleeping. So after three months of this, I knew we were going to have to discuss the situation and make some changes or I would have to pack my bags and move out.

2. Write your own narrative paragraph relating an incident that led to your making a compromise with another person. Pay careful attention to the details you select to describe the incident and the sequence in which you present the details.

Other Modes of Development

By now you can see that constructing an essay is a step-by-step process in which each step builds upon the previous one. Brainstorming helps you envision your response to an exam question and structure your ideas into a scratch outline. In your introduction, you follow through with your outline by summarizing your main points in a thesis and by setting up a plan for the essay in your road map. Your road map also establishes a sequence for your body paragraphs; then your body paragraphs follow the plan, developing and supporting your thesis. Each body paragraph deals with a different aspect of or different idea related to your thesis. Without brainstorming, you will have no material to develop your essay; without a thesis, you will have no purpose or focus for your essay; without a plan, you will have no direction for your essay.

Once you have generated and organized information in response to an exam question and formulated a thesis and plan, you must develop the essay's body paragraphs. Just as you looked for cues (key and directional words) in your exam question to help you determine your topic and your response, you can also use these cues to determine your approach. Exam questions may suggest—or even require—information in a certain format. As you have seen, narration is a common format used to present details that support a point. In addition, an exam question that asks you, for example, to discuss benefits and drawbacks suggests **comparison.** Other types of questions may ask you to **explain a process** or **analyze causes and effects.**

For most exam questions you'll need to develop ideas in different modes. For example, you may have to **narrate** an incident, then use **cause/effect analysis** to determine why events happened as they did, and **compare** the incident with another that turned out differently. Thus, a writer could use three different modes to develop three paragraphs. These modes provide a structure to guide a writer in composing paragraphs. Understanding the guidelines for writing in different modes will give you a strategy for developing paragraphs that are more organized, detailed, and relevant to your exam question.

Comparison

To compare is to point out similarities between two or more items; to contrast is to point out differences. We usually refer to this mode as **comparison.** Sometimes on proficiency exams these comparisons center on before-and-after situations: you may be asked to discuss a turning point in your life, a time when you acted differently than you normally do, how you have changed since entering college, or how a friend has changed during your relationship. You may also be asked to compare your views on a subject with those of someone who opposes you or to analyze the benefits and drawbacks of a law or regulation. The "Castle of Chillon" essay question suggested a comparison: Discuss the relationship between life learning and formal education.

On essay exams in most subjects, comparison is an effective way for students to display their knowledge. You may have to compare dissimilar theories, such as evolution versus creation; religious creeds, such as Judaism and Christianity; civilizations, such as Aztecs and Mayans or Ancient Romans and Ancient Greeks; methods, such as fly fishing and bait fishing; or presidents, such as Jimmy Carter and Ronald Reagan. For any exam question that requires comparison, you will examine two (or more) elements in relation to certain criteria that either *you* must establish or your exam question will require. These criteria are important; you can't cover *all* the likenesses and differences between Carter and Reagan, for example, in a two-hour exam. So if your topic does not limit what you should write about, *you* must: "Although Presidents Jimmy Carter and Ronald Reagan both had limited experience in politics before being elected, their foreign policy and economic policy greatly differed." This statement, which limits your discussion to the two presidents' political experience, foreign policy, and economic policy, could serve as either a thesis statement for your essay (if your question required *only* the comparison), or a unifying idea for a paragraph (if the question also required other tasks, such as analyzing what caused the two presidents to differ).

Your brainstorming will help you to identify and select criteria to use in making a comparison. One effective approach is to start your brainstorming by writing down the elements or items you are comparing at the top of a page with a vertical line between them. Then as you write an idea in one column, make a similar comment in the other column(s). This process will assure that your comparison is *balanced*, that you are examining the *same points of comparison* for each element being compared. For example, if, in your "Carter" column, you wrote "served one term as Governor of Georgia before being elected president," you would make a similar comment in your "Reagan" column: "served two terms as Governor of California before being elected president." Also, in both columns you would note "had no experience in the Senate or the Assembly." In some comparisons you may have more to say about one element being compared than the other, but you should acknowledge the *same points* in both elements being compared so your reader can easily follow the comparison. A comparison that mentions different points for each element being compared is confusing and illogical.

Notice how balanced and thorough the writer is in the following paragraphs about a major turning point in her life, the birth of her child. Also notice how she uses specific detail coupled with analysis to make her points. The unifying idea is in **bold type,** and main supporting points, or subtopic sentences, are <u>underlined</u> (subtopic sentences are explained in Chapter 4, page 62).

"Turning Point"

Before my daughter was born, my life was very carefree. By carefree, I mean that many of my activities were spontaneous and I wasn't overly concerned with household chores. <u>First of all, I hardly ever planned activities, but we were always on the go.</u> Sometimes my husband and I would jump in the car and end up in the mountains somewhere. Once we went on a simple Sunday drive and ended up spending three days at our friend's cabin on the lake. Other times friends would come over; before we knew it, we had a great party going. Whenever I felt like it, I could go shopping all day or stay out all night; it didn't matter because the only person I had to worry about was myself. Also, I didn't worry about mundane household responsibilities like shopping for food or cleaning. If we were out of food, we'd just go out to eat. Nor did it matter if the dishes didn't get washed or the bed made; household tidiness wasn't an important factor in my life.

      After my daughter arrived, my life changed drastically; I had to be more responsible. Activities now had to be carefully planned, and in order to function efficiently, I had to keep the house in order. I now became acutely aware of planning and scheduling. Car trips even just across town required packing the "baby bag" with "just-in-case" extras— food, clothes, diapers, toys, etc. Friends had to be gone or I had to be home by 9:00 p.m. because I had to be up by 6:00 a.m. Shopping was a major excursion now, and something I hardly ever did unless I first hired a babysitter. In addition, taking care of the household was critical in keeping our lives running smoothly. Since outings required planning and extra cash, eating out became a special occasion, so we always had to have food on hand. In fact, for the first six months, we went out to dinner only once—on our anniversary. Dishes had to be done regularly since I often bathed the baby in the kitchen sink. Making the bed was the one thing I continued to neglect—after all, it only got messed up every night anyway.

Another feature that makes the "Turning Point" paragraphs proficient is organization: the writer covered the points of comparison—activities and household responsibilities—in the same sequence in both paragraphs. This careful organization not only makes her ideas much easier to follow, but also makes the before-and-after differences even more obvious and convincing.

The author of the "Turning Point" paragraphs chose the **Block Method** of organization for her comparison, in which she organized her ideas in blocks of information by *ideas being compared:* the two ideas she is comparing are *her life before* and *her life after* the turning point. Another method you can use to organize a comparison is the **Point-by-Point Method.** In this method you organize details by *main points of comparison.* The *main points* of comparison in the "Turning

Point" paragraphs are *activities* and *household chores*. Had the author chosen the point-by-point method of comparison, she would have discussed all her details about activities in one paragraph and all her details about household responsibilities in the other, alternating between "before" and "after" in each paragraph. Here are outlines of the Block and the Point-by-Point Methods of organizing comparison paragraphs.

   Deciding which method to use is up to you. Some topics are best handled with a point-by-point comparison, while others are more clear when the elements being compared are dealt with separately. The Point-by-Point Method is best for longer comparisons. When you have a number of points to compare, the Point-by-Point Method will enable you to discuss the various points separately, thus keeping a clear focus on the *points of comparison*. For example, in an essay comparing soccer and football, your points of

BLOCK METHOD

Idea A	Before Daughter's Birth

Main Point 1
   Support details
	Spontaneous Activities
	   Sunday drives
	   Impromptu parties
	   Shopping trips
	   Late nights out

Main Point 2
   Support details
	Neglected Household Chores
	   Forgot grocery shopping/often ate out
	   Dishes not done
	   Bed not made

Idea B	After Daughter's Birth

Main Point 1
   Support details
	Planned Activities
	   Car trips
	   Visits with friends
	   Shopping trips

Main Point 2
   Support details
	Had To Do Household Chores
	   Regular grocery shopping/
	      hardly ever ate out
	   Dishes done/baby's bath
	   Bed still not made

POINT-BY-POINT METHOD

Main Point 1	**Activities Changed**

Idea A
  Support details
	Before — Spontaneous
	    Car trips
	    Visits with friends
	    Shopping trips

Idea B
  Support details
	After — Planned
	    Car trips
	    Visits with friends
	    Shopping trips

Main Point 2	**Household Chores Changed**

Idea A
  Support details
	Before — Neglected
	    Forgot to buy food/ate out often
	    Didn't wash dishes
	    Didn't fix bed

Idea B
  Support details
	After — Did Regularly
	    Bought food weekly/few meals out
	    Had to wash dishes/baby's bath
	    Still didn't make bed

comparison might be player positions, game rules, equipment, and strategies. A Point-by-Point comparison would enable you to thoroughly discuss each of these points in a separate paragraph. On the other hand, the Block Method focuses on the *ideas being compared;* usually each idea is dealt with in a separate paragraph. This method is best for *shorter* comparisons, or at least, comparisons with fewer points to compare. The Block Method permits you to elaborate on a particular point that might be important to one side of the comparison but is not as significant to another side. For example, in the "Turning Point" paragraphs, the writer did not have much to say about household chores in her "before" paragraph, but gave much more detail about her household responsibilities in her "after" paragraph. Often your purpose for making the comparison and the details you want to include in the comparison will help you determine which method to use. Therefore, you should brainstorm *before* you select a comparison format, then choose the one that best suits your writing situation and the details you have generated for the essay.

Proficient writers realize that the key to an effective comparison—whether it be a few paragraphs in an essay or the entire essay—is organization and balance. You should not confuse readers with details that seem out of place or points that are mentioned about one side of the comparison but not about the other. In an effective comparison, similarities and differences are easy to distinguish, and the purpose of the comparison is clear.

EXERCISE 6-2

1. Brainstorm ideas for a comparison on ONE of the following: the teaching styles of two instructors you have had, two types of music, two sports you enjoy watching or playing, two leaders you are familiar with, *or* two fast-food restaurants. Remember to balance your points of comparison. Then use the *Point-by-Point Method* to organize your details into an outline.
2. Now organize your details into an outline using the *Block Method*.
3. Which method do you think works best for your comparison? Why?

Process Analysis

A **process analysis** relates steps *in a sequence* undertaken to complete a task. There are two kinds of process analyses: *Instructional writing*, which tells a reader *how to do something;* and *informational writing*, which tells a reader *how something occurs.* Typically, your process analysis will focus on a kind of *informational writing*—telling a reader *how something happened.* For example, on essay exams, you may be asked to relate what you did to reach a goal or break a bad habit, explain what you did to teach someone how to perform a task, or describe an inefficient procedure. Or you may have to discuss the stages of a physical or mental illness or how acid rain harms the environment. In all of these cases, you will be recounting the steps in a process. A process explanation is like narration because the temporal sequence provides structure for the paragraph, and steps related out of sequence can confuse a reader.

Most procedures occur in sequential order; one step must be completed before the next can begin.[1] Therefore, the most effective

---

[1] When a process requires performing certain steps, but there is no fixed order or sequence for these steps, you can present the steps in the "order of choice" — the sequence *you* feel is most efficient or appropriate.

organization is **the chronological order.** Your brainstorming notes should have a list or cluster on the process, although at the brainstorming stage, the list may be in random order. As you read it over, first make sure you have not omitted any critical step or action involved in the procedure; then arrange the information in the order the steps occur.

As you arrange your information, you will probably notice that several small steps are involved in completing one more predominant *phase*. (For example, brainstorming, organizing your brainstorming notes, and compiling a scratch outline are smaller steps in the larger *planning phase* of essay composition.) As your outline begins to take shape, you will want to *name* your main phases and arrange minor steps under each main phase. This organizing process will help you later. As you construct your paragraph, you will mention each main phase as a *sub-idea* or subtopic sentence, which supports your paragraph's unifying idea or main idea. Your unifying idea should not only mention the process you are explaining, but also *your point of view or attitude toward the process:* "The victims of Alzheimer's disease degenerate in a slow but grueling manner"; "A peace officer must follow the arrest procedure carefully for the arrest to be valid." Finally, a good process analysis explains *why* one step occurs after another: "I had to actually count the number of cigarettes I smoked each day before I could devise a plan to cut back on my smoking."

The following example shows how a writer used this organized approach to discuss what he did to break a bad habit. He began by brainstorming; then he organized and categorized his notes by phases. Next, he wrote a sentence that expressed his main idea and subtopic sentences that named each phase. Finally, he wrote his paragraph. First read the exam question carefully; the portion that requires process analysis is underlined.

> Identify a bad habit you have and discuss what you did (or are doing) to break it. Then analyze why you have or have not been successful in eliminating the bad habit.

Now here is the paragraph the student composed. The **unifying idea** is in **boldface,** and subtopic sentences are underlined.

> **Breaking my bad habit of smoking was a gradual but rewarding process.** The first phase of my process to break my smoking habit involved reducing the number of

<u>cigarettes I smoked each day.</u> I started by counting the number of cigarettes I smoked each day for a week. Then I made a chart of how many I would allow myself to smoke each day over the next two weeks. Following the chart wasn't easy, but I managed to cut back an average of one cigarette a day over the previous day. I was already feeling good about myself. <u>The next phase of my program involved behavior modification.</u> During the fourth week, I noted times and circumstances when I had a cigarette craving. This led me to rescheduling or eliminating certain activities that led me to smoke. For example, I began eating breakfast *before* I took a shower, so I had something to do immediately after eating besides smoking. Not having as many chances to smoke cut my habit down to four or five cigarettes a day. My life was improving. <u>Now I was ready for Phase 3—to stop completely.</u> So I threw out all my smoking paraphernalia, even the lighter in my car! And whenever I went out to eat, I proudly asked to sit in the non-smoking section. I refused to allow others to smoke in my home and began to enjoy smoke-free air. Although I stopped buying cigarettes, I occasionally borrowed one from a friend. But when I was down to two a week, I knew I had my habit almost kicked.

Note how this paragraph explains the process thoroughly in chronological order, using subtopic sentences to mark each phase. Also note how the supporting details focus on the process as being *gradual* and *rewarding*. The writer has adequately addressed the part of the question that involves process explanation, but his essay is not complete; he must have a paragraph identifying and describing the bad habit before the paragraph explaining the process and one paragraph following the process explanation analyzing why he was successful in breaking his bad habit. He has used the process analysis mode to develop one of several paragraphs in this essay.

EXERCISE 6-3

Develop a *process analysis paragraph* for the following proficiency exam question. Begin by brainstorming and dividing your information into main phases. Then write a subtopic sentence for each phase. When writing your paragraph, <u>underline</u> your unifying idea and each subtopic sentence.

Discuss a situation in which you had to teach someone something. Then analyze what you learned from this teaching experience.

Cause/Effect

Developing paragraphs in an essay through the cause/effect mode requires more analysis than the other modes mentioned here. For example, a process analysis simply describes the stages in a process; a cause/effect analysis tries to explain the relationship between the stages or determine *why* one stage necessarily follows another. Or, a narrative relates a series of events; cause/effect analysis explores *why* the events occurred. You are examining not only what happened, but also *why* or *how* it happened as it did, and *what* the consequences were: the causes of a certain event or occurrence and the effects or repercussions. The cause/effect mode may be combined with one or more of the other modes to develop paragraphs in your essay. Sometimes you may be asked to write on just the causes or just the effects: what causes you to become frustrated and depressed, what causes a certain social problem, the effects of living in today's fast-paced society, the effects of a political decision, the effects of television on children. More often, though, you will be asked to examine *both* the causes and effects—a kind of "before-and-after" analysis, with the causes being the "before" and the effects being the "after." In fact, sometimes it is difficult to separate the two: the effects are the natural consequences of the causes. For example, if you were asked to write about a serious problem that modern society faces, you would probably want to discuss both the causes of this problem and the adverse effects it has on society. Acquired Immune Deficiency Syndrome (AIDS) would be a very appropriate subject to write about for this topic. If you chose to write about the impact AIDS has had on lifestyles, you'd have to consider the causes of the disease (or how people contract it) in order to examine the effects (or lifestyle changes Americans have made). Sometimes when examining the causes and effects of a problem, you discover a solution or a method to curb the problem's severity, which can be a natural way of concluding a cause/effect analysis.

If your task is to write about *just* causes or *just* effects, your brainstorming is already focused; you must, however, be thorough. A good guideline to follow would be to keep asking yourself "why" after each thought that comes to you. For example, here is how one writer generated information for a paragraph on what caused her to become frustrated and depressed:

What causes me to become frustrated and depressed?

Heavy work and school load. Why? No time for myself. Why is that a problem? I can't do things I want to do, like go sailing or spend a weekend in the mountains or go out dancing with friend after work. Why? I have to spend free time studying. Why? I want to do well in school. Why? I want a good job when I graduate, not the dead-end one I have. Why? I want to be successful so I'll have a better life. Why? Because my life right now is difficult and I feel trapped. Why? Because I can't do the things I want to do—can't afford to and have no time to. Why? Because my present job where I work 40 hours a week pays only $750 per month which is barely enough to cover all my expenses.

This brainstorming has yielded many interwoven causes for the writer's frustration and depression, all of which relate to her lack of free time. Just asking "why" reveals a causal chain; the writer could discuss the entire chain of reasons, or focus on one or two ideas in the chain.

When an essay question asks you to examine *both* causes and effects, you can take a brainstorming approach similar to the one used to generate information for a comparison. That is, you may want to draw a vertical line down the center of a blank piece of paper and write "causes" on one side and "effects" on the other. As you write down a cause, try to think of an effect related to it, and vice versa; often effects logically flow out of causes. If a situation, or cause, has *several* repercussions, or effects, or if a certain problem was the result of several causes, be sure to list these ideas together. You can later use these groups of related ideas to formulate paragraphs.

Here is an example of how a student used cause-effect analysis to generate information for an essay about a serious problem facing society:

QUESTION:
Analyze a serious problem facing American society.

Acquired Immune Deficiency Syndrome (AIDS) is a serious problem in the United States today.

Causes				Effects
Sexual Contact	=	AIDS	=	People are scared
				People are abstaining from sex
				More people are becoming monogamous
				People are less promiscuous
				People are using condoms
Transfusions	=	AIDS	=	HIV test for all blood donations
				Families storing their "safe" blood
				People are refusing transfusions
I.V. Drug Use	=	AIDS	=	Public health campaigns to "clean your works"
				Clinics give out free hypodermic needles
				Some people are happy because the disease eliminates drug users

The disease is in the middle of this causal chain—AIDS is what links the causes to the effects. For example, AIDS is both the EFFECT of sexual contact, and the CAUSE of people being scared. This student's next step would be to develop each cause/effect group into a paragraph, providing explanations and examples to support his main ideas.

Cause/effect is an appropriate mode to consider when your exam topic or essay question asks for analysis. This mode provides a structure for discussing both the origins of a situation and the consequences or results. Whether you are considering just the causes, just the effects, or both, you must present your ideas in a logical order, or your analysis will seem weak and nonproficient.

Some exam questions may require multiple tasks; others may suggest one particular approach. In either case, you must be organized and thorough. Therefore, you should analyze your exam topic carefully to determine exactly how to develop your response. Understanding the guidelines for writing narratives, comparisons, process analyses, and cause/effect analyses will help you structure your paragraphs (and your entire essay) more proficiently.

EXERCISE 6-4

In the following paragraph identify the causes and resulting effects of the student's frustration and depression. First underline the causes and effects, then list them side by side.

> Working full time and trying to handle an 18-unit school load cause me to become depressed and frustrated. My extremely busy schedule leaves me with little time to relax, which results in my feeling very unhappy and dissatisfied with my life. First of all, a full-time job is time-consuming under any circumstances. However, I often have to work overtime, which decreases my free time even further. As a result, I have little time to spend with my family. In addition, this lack of time causes me to neglect my household responsibilities; dishes don't get done for days on end, my bed is never made, and I don't like to think about what could be growing in the bathroom! This lack of time and resulting disorganization also effect my punctuality. I am often late for important appointments, if I even remember to show up at all. As if work weren't enough, I also carry an 18-unit load in college, which results in even less free time and even more frustration. Course assignments bring me to the library after work almost every evening. Early morning classes require me to be up at the crack of dawn. To keep up this pace, some nights I get only three or four hours of sleep. These effects of my heavy work and school load are taking their toll on me.

EXERCISE 6-5

Determine the various modes you could use to develop paragraphs for the following exam topics. Begin by identifying the directional words.

1. Analyze a procedure that you feel is inefficient. Explain the procedure and discuss its resulting inadequacies. Then point out measures you feel could be taken to improve the procedure's efficiency.

2. Describe your parents' disciplinary practices as you were growing up. Explain the effects that their discipline had on your life and how you feel about it today, as an adult. Finally, discuss how the discipline you received as a child will or does affect you as a parent disciplining your own children.

Consider the practices you will imitate and those you will change or eliminate.

3. Today we are discovering many negative or even harmful effects of technological advances we once thought were beneficial to society. Identify such a technological advance and discuss the intended benefits and the resulting drawbacks.

PROVIDING TRANSITIONS

Understanding the different writing modes enables you to develop organized approaches to writing parts of or an entire essay, and this organization is important to writing proficiency. However, sometimes organization is not enough. Proficient writing must also have a sense of flow or continuity; without it, even the most well organized ideas may seem unrelated and, therefore, confusing. **Transitions** establish this continuity.

In reading a story, article, or essay, have you ever been confused about why one sentence followed another or why the paragraphs were arranged in a certain order? Or in reading a paragraph, have you noticed an irritating sense of abruptness or choppiness, as if the sentences were not related in any way or the thoughts expressed were independent of each other? This kind of writing is nonproficient; it is tedious and unpleasant to read, and it puts the burden of understanding sequence on the reader. Proficient writing employs continuity—smooth, logical movement from one thought to the next, from one main idea to the next. Writers achieve this continuity by using **transitions**—both within paragraphs to link individual sentences, and between paragraphs, to link main ideas.

Transitions are related to modes of development because each mode provides an implicit structure for the essay, and effective transitions can remind the reader of this structure. Regardless of the mode you choose to organize your ideas, regardless of how well developed and organized your paragraphs or essays may be, without transition, your ideas may seem disjointed or choppy.

Transitions within Paragraphs

Transitions are needed within paragraphs to connect thoughts expressed in individual sentences. Providing these transitions is a way of leading a reader step by step through your thoughts—a way of indicating how individual thoughts are associated. For example, in the following paragraph, the writer failed to provide transitions, even though events he expresses are definitely related. The paragraph sounds like a list—as if the events are separate items. As you read it, also consider the impression this paragraph gives you of the writer:

"Bad Day"

My alarm didn't go off. I got up late. I couldn't eat breakfast. I had no time. I just got dressed. I ran to the bus stop. The bus pulled away before I got there. I was late for work. Today was going to be a bad day.

At best, this paragraph suggests that the writer has little concern for his audience—he seems to think readers don't mind a long series of short, choppy sentences. At worst, this paragraph gives readers the impression that the writer is very unsophisticated—almost simple-minded. The paragraph sounds like a passage from a fourth-grade reader! Combining several short sentences into longer ones would help make this paragraph more readable. Linking those longer sentences with transitions would make the paragraph flow.

Writers who provide transitions are aware that readers may need help in making associations between sentences. Transitions provide these connections for readers, thus establishing a sense of flow and logic. Readers do not have to guess if one sentence is a result or consequence of a previous one, if another sentence is a contrast to an adjacent sentence, or if a sentence expands upon or continues the thought expressed in the one before. Through transitions, the writer has thoughtfully provided these connections.

One method of establishing transition between sentences uses a special group of words called **transitional markers.** These words, which usually appear at the beginning of a sentence, "mark" or suggest the kind of information that the rest of the sentence will express: *a continuation* or *extension, a contrast, an illustration, a conclusion* or *result, a series* or *time sequence.*

Here is a list of common transitional markers categorized by their function:

Addition/Continuation

furthermore
moreover
also
in addition
besides
in other words
another

Time/Space Sequence

first, second, etc.
next
then
finally

Contrast

however
nevertheless
although
but
yet
though

Result/Conclusion

therefore
consequently
as a result
thus
in conclusion
accordingly
finally
because of

Example

for example
that is
for instance

You don't want to begin *every* sentence with a transitional marker. Using them selectively to introduce a sentence that immediately follows and is logically related to another sentence will provide a junction readers sometimes need to make reading smooth and understanding clear.

Here is a revised version of the paragraph on the "Bad Day," with sentences combined and transitions added. Note how much smoother *and* more proficient the paragraph sounds. The transitional markers are underlined.

Revised

"Bad Day"

Today would be a bad day for me. My alarm didn't go off, so I got up late. <u>Furthermore</u>, since I had no time, I couldn't eat breakfast. I just got dressed and ran to the bus stop. <u>Nevertheless</u>, the bus pulled away before I got there; <u>as a result</u>, I was late for work!

[Note: Sentences are often linked with transitional markers by putting a semicolon at the end of the first independent clause, then beginning the second independent clause with the transitional marker; a comma usually comes immediately after the transitional marker. See Chapter 10 for more information on punctuating sentences.]

Transitions between Paragraphs

Proficient writers also take care to provide links between paragraphs in an essay so that readers understand the relationship of the essay parts. Transitions between paragraphs help readers to understand paragraph sequence and to distinguish the writer's support ideas. Paragraphs should not be isolated units; they should be clearly bound by the essay's thesis. Transitions between paragraphs connect the unifying idea of one paragraph with the unifying idea of the next. Paragraphs should not be presented as separate from each other; writers need to link these parts to each other and to the thesis.

Depending upon the mode(s) you are using to develop your paragraphs, transition may come naturally. For example, referring to the contrast in ideas would be an easy way to link two comparison paragraphs (see the "before" and "after" sample comparison paragraphs on pages 93–94); discussing causes in one paragraph and following that discussion with an effects paragraph that refers to the causes would be an obvious way to provide transition between these two. When paragraphs have no apparent connection, you should reread topic sentences of the paragraphs you want to link, looking for key words. You can then use those key words in a phrase or sentence at either *the end of one paragraph* to introduce the next, or at *the beginning of a new paragraph* to refer to the previous paragraph. Here are some examples. Key words are in **bold type;** transitional sentences are <u>underlined.</u>

1. Provide transition at the <u>end</u> of one paragraph as a way of leading into the next paragraph.

One technique **advertisers** use to get the **public's attention** is to show **scenic views.** Cigarette advertisements often show pictures of lush forests, wild horses running across a plain, or free-flowing mountain streams, with a quick message of "smoke ours" printed on the bottom. Beer advertisements are set in the wilderness; soft drink ads often show young people lazily lounging on a tropical beach. But if the **beautiful countryside** won't get the **public's attention,** the **beautiful people** will.

A second **advertising** ploy to get **consumers' attention** is to parade **attractive people** who swear by a certain product before the public's eyes. For example, women in shampoo advertisements not only have thick, flowing hair, but also have perfect make-up, slender figures and fashionable clothes. Men in toothpaste advertisements are clean-shaven and bright-eyed as they stand before the mirror to brush their teeth in the morning. Even the children in cereal advertisements are adorable and perfectly groomed.

2. Provide transition at the beginning of a paragraph by referring to the idea in the paragraph immediately before.

Often **animal names** are used to characterize a **person** with some **peculiarity** or **unpleasant quality**. A stupid or foolish person is called an "ass," a "donkey," or a "baboon." Cowards are called "chickens," and the very passive are referred to as "sheep." A sloppy person is a "pig," and a greedy person a "hog." A sly person is a "fox" or a "weasel."

However, though these **animal names** may define **unpleasant human qualities** , they are not "fair" to the animals. Pigs, for example, are not sloppy, nor is a baboon stupid. Foxes may be able to run quickly, but they are not particularly sly, and hogs are hungry—but not necessarily greedy.

3. Use "another" to link main ideas.

One characteristic of an effective teacher is patience. A good teacher must realize that sometimes learning is a slow process; therefore, he or she must be able to calmly explain a concept as many times as necessary until every student understands. A good teacher also understands that some assignments take longer than others and should be willing to extend due dates for students having difficulty with an assignment. When a teacher is patient with students, the students will not feel threatened and will develop confidence in their ability to learn.

Another characteristic of an effective teacher is a sense of humor. Humor is a way of breaking the ice with students; when they can laugh, they feel comfortable, and when they feel comfortable, they will be more open to learning. Also, humor is a way for a teacher to communicate concepts more effectively: students may remember a humorous story related to an important concept more easily than they will a serious lecture, because humor makes the concept more fun.

The third method of establishing transition, using "another," is certainly not the most effective way to link ideas, but it is better than *no transition* at all. It is a writer's responsibility to keep readers on track by providing transition within and between paragraphs. Ultimately, this transition will leave the readers with an overall sense of unity and a much clearer understanding of the writer's ideas.

EXERCISE 6-6

Use transitional markers to provide links between the following sentences.

1. I had to work overtime. I was unable to study for my final in chemistry. I failed it. I passed the class.
2. The man in the plaid shirt and striped pants is quite wealthy. He still shops at thrift stores for all his clothes. He thinks he looks quite fashionable.
3. We were very hungry. Our waiter ignored us for thirty minutes. He brought us the wrong food. I didn't leave him a tip.
4. She turned the lights down low. She put on soft, romantic music. She poured the wine into special crystal glasses. Kevin did not propose.
5. Dr. Applegate gave the math students explicit instructions on how to solve the complex algebra problem. He expected them all to get the problem right on the test. Most of them got it wrong.

SUMMARY

1. Avoid using narration, particularly unreflective narration, as the *primary* mode for developing an essay.

2. When using narration, be careful to employ a clear organization—usually chronological. Take care not to write sentences that simply announce an event at the beginning of narrative paragraphs; focus on the point the narration is making. Make sure each paragraph contains some analysis, evaluation, or judgment of the event or situation. Omit details that occurred in chronological order but are not relevant to the controlling idea.

3. When using comparison to develop paragraphs (or an entire essay), compare related ideas. Balance your comparison by matching subtopics for each element in the comparison.

4. When using process analysis to develop paragraphs, follow a careful plan of organization (usually chronological) to present the steps, so your reader can easily understand what is involved. Don't omit important steps. Try to group smaller, related steps into main phases; consider devoting a separate paragraph to each phase.

5. Develop cause and effect paragraphs thoroughly and analytically. When appropriate, align causes and effects. Remember some causes may have several effects and vice versa.

6. Analyze exam topics carefully to determine which modes are appropriate for your response. Remember that writing thorough essays may require employing several modes.

7. Provide transitions between sentences within a paragraph and between paragraphs in an essay to establish continuity and link ideas for readers.

Constructing Conclusions and Checking Your Essay

Most proficient writers know that a good essay comes to a definite end, so they are careful to include a concluding paragraph. Even after you have been writing for two hours, a concluding paragraph indicates to the reader that you are still in control of your essay, that your ideas remain related, and that you have indeed planned carefully.

What you learned in the chapter on Rules of Thumb (Chapter 2) is critical here. Writing a conclusion and checking your essay form a crucial part of planning your response—you absolutely **must** allot some time (even 15 to 20 minutes) to make sure that you do both. In fact, it would be better to leave a planned body paragraph somewhat incomplete (or even omit it entirely) in order to have those critical minutes for concluding and checking.

Everyone likes to know when something has ended: it is just human. We look forward to the ends of television shows, airplane flights, presidential administrations, movies, baseball games—even to great works of art, such as symphonies, long poems, novels, and plays. Whether it is the climax where the criminals are apprehended, the slowing from 600 mph and descent into New York, the lame duck period, the ninth inning, or the denouement, we all note telltale signs that cue and comfort us that the end is here—and that we have experienced something unified. A good conclusion to an essay serves many of those same purposes. On the other hand, omissions such as leaving off a concluding paragraph or letting your essay end while you are still scribbling details in a body paragraph leave readers disappointed and suggest a lack of proficiency.

It may seem obvious that you should write a conclusion, but much of importance is discovered by investigating what seems obvious. Your conclusion is the last part of your essay that graders will read. If graders are still in doubt as to whether your writing is proficient or not, they will often make that judgment based on your concluding paragraph. You have probably noticed by now that though all of us approach some level of consistency in evaluating writing, evaluation is a subtle and subjective process—there are no absolutes. The graders may wonder while reading your essay whether to pass you. And they may still be undecided at the end, looking for a firm cue or reason to be swayed one way or the other. Don't let a missing or inadequate conclusion lower your grade or lead to failure!

AVOID ESSAYESE

Students often begin their concluding paragraph with the words "In conclusion" or "To conclude" or even "Thus we have seen" or "In this essay I have. . . ." While these phrases may satisfy some readers and work as a handy reminder to some writers, most readers will view them as mechanical and obvious. In effect, these words simply constitute another bit of **essayese** (see Chapter 5) to avoid.

You have noticed already that most formal aspects of writing depend on subtle cues to the reader, for example, the several spaces of indentation that mark a paragraph, the punctuation that separates one sentence from another or suggests critical divisions within the sentence. For the same reasons, you want your conclusion to declare itself to the reader with subtle cues. Just as you would not begin a body paragraph with the phrase "Here is body paragraph #3," you should not begin your concluding paragraph with essayese.

You should also avoid other forms of essayese within the paragraph itself. Using the conclusion simply to repeat word for word the thesis and road map in your introduction reeks of essayese. Most readers (including you) know when your concluding paragraph is merely a *pro forma* bundle of words; use the conclusion to show the reader there is a thinking mind behind those words. All approaches that involve essayese bore a reader and suggest that you do not have much facility in writing or ability to manipulate ideas. Here is an example of a weak conclusion using mechanical strategies. We have given you the question and introduction so you can see how little the conclusion advances the essay's main ideas:

QUESTION

Write an essay in which, drawing from your personal experience, knowledge and observations, you analyze a procedure that you believe is inefficient—and discuss what you think could be done to make it more efficient.

I1 — Introduction

Are students being taught to study efficiently? It's easy for a teacher to throw a textbook and a syllabus in front of a student and say, "Read chapters 1, 2, and 3. Come back next Monday, and I'll lecture on them." The student is expected to go home, digest the material, and return Monday to be enlightened by the professor. There is a mid-term exam, and then a final at the end of the course, and on these the student is expected to regurgitate the material. The typical professor never offers the student advice on study habits. This pattern is exactly what I have observed in my fellow students for the past four years: these students get assignments, digest them and regurgitate them. But then, just as quickly, students forget what they have learned. <u>If teachers were to introduce study techniques to their classes, students would learn efficiently and retain the information.</u> Teachers could explain how to create a record and study sheet by careful note-taking <A>, could suggest occasionally reading similar material in other texts and professional journals to reinforce the information <B>, and could provide review sessions in which they encourage students to imagine challenging exam questions <C>.

C1-A—Nonproficient Conclusion

In conclusion, I have shown that students are not now being taught to study efficiently. Currently they are expected to go home, digest the lecture material, and return Monday to be enlightened by the professor. But in this essay we have seen that, if teachers were to introduce study techniques to their classes, students would learn efficiently and retain the information. So, if teachers could explain note-taking, would suggest reading similar material, and would provide review sessions in which they encouraged students to imagine challenging exam questions, students would study more effectively.

CONCLUDING STRATEGIES

But what *should* you do? You want to write a final paragraph that brings matters to a close; but you should not repeat the thesis verbatim, and you should not simply tell the reader "here is the conclusion." What you need is a variety of strategies for writing proficient conclusions. Many strategies can work; here are five that may help you:

Restatement

Epitome example

Analogy

Complement to introduction

Prediction or Extension

Restatement

Rather than merely repeating your thesis and road map, you could restate them in a variety of ways, rearranging the material or paraphrasing what you wrote in the introduction. Remember, though, that to keep your essay unified, you need to echo key words from the question and your thesis—changing *all* your terms at this point would confuse a reader.

Let's examine how we might use a concluding paragraph to restate and rework the thesis and road map from Introduction 1:

C1-B—Proficient Conclusion

> Once students begin to imagine their own exam questions, to challenge themselves, they are far better prepared to study efficiently and perform well on exams. Even if an exam question is not what they expect, they have already redigested the course information on their own, and much more of it is available to them in a spontaneous way as they write on the new topic. Of course, they are also far better prepared to take the exam because they have studied alternate approaches to the material through collateral reading in other texts and in professional journals. And they need not cram relentlessly to remember the professor's lectures or the assigned reading because they have been trained in proficient note-taking techniques all through the course. So, if a professor would only take a few hours out of the semester to train his students in study techniques, they would not only avoid the typical cram-regurgitation process of finals—they would also be well on their way to using the material later in a variety of settings.

Notice how this conclusion uses essentially the same materials as the introduction. It echoes key words **(instructor, study techniques, imagine, exam questions, reading, note-taking),** but it does not mechanically reproduce sentences or ideas. The conclusion begins, naturally enough, with Topic <C> of the introduction—as this would be the topic of the last body paragraph. It works backward through the road map, in order to show the reader how new study techniques help prepare a student for a final exam. Ultimately, in the last sentence, it goes beyond the focus on the finals. A reader can see that this conclusion has benefited from the developing of the essay's unifying idea that has taken place in the body paragraphs. This conclusion helps the reader remember the essay's main points as well as offering a slightly new perspective—but, clearly, *not* a perspective that *contradicts* the thesis or the essay.

Epitome Example

Just as you can begin your essay with an anecdote or a description, so you can end your essay with concrete details which show that your unifying idea works. In effect, you are offering another example—just as you might in a body paragraph. Yet this example should be chosen with care. It should be an **epitome**—an example that functions as a symbol or that embodies or represents a whole class of examples. Here is such a conclusion written for the same topic as the introduction above:

> As I prepared to write my final exam for a class in contemporary American film, I had imagined writing about questions on the role of women in contemporary film; or a comparison of revisionist Westerns with Westerns of the 30s, 40s, and 50s; or an analysis of Weir's *Witness*. Instead, I faced a question asking me to discuss Verhoeven's *Robocop*. But I could still use my imagined questions to develop this one: I could use my role-of-women analysis to comment on the unusual woman-partner for Robocop; I could use my analysis of Westerns to show *Robocop*'s transfer of the good/evil mythology of a pastoral landscape to a rough, futuristic urban one, and I could even use my observations on *Witness* to comment on the dehumanizing threat of mechanization, the salvation via a borderline character partaking of both man and machine. I could also use parallel reading in Kolker's *A Cinema of Loneliness*. Using an efficient study procedure here, rather than cramming for the exam, would make a dramatic improvement in higher education. It would also lead to students emerging from their final exams as more sophisticated learners, in this case proud of their abilities as critics of films, more than bored or listless readers of movie ads in the daily newspapers.

Notice that this writer has used her personal experience of studying for and taking the final exam in a particular course as an **epitome** to illustrate the effectiveness of two of the three study techniques. Even though the approach is concrete, the concluding paragraph reminds the reader of **key words** from the question (efficient procedure) and key concepts from the essay, as well as providing a kind of "final proof" that the writer's thesis may be valid.

Analogy

Just as you may use analogy to stimulate readers' imaginations in an introduction, so you may use it in a conclusion to leave them with a forceful image at the end of your essay. In a way, you are still rearranging the basic building blocks of thesis and road map to make a final impression. Sometimes your specific idea can be made clearer by comparing it to a concept the reader is more familiar with. Remember, to create an analogy, first state the subject of your essay; follow with the phrase "is like"; then finish the sentence. Consider the analogy developed here, written in response to Question 2, Chapter 5, page 68. The essay begins with descriptive detail in the introductory paragraph:

I2 — Introduction

Workers are paid based on what they are worth, on their hours of preparation, on how the "market" values their job, on their years of education — in other words, salaries are based on some rational system. Right? No, wrong! There is no rational basis for any system of salaries. A talented observer can always detect inequities and arbitrary standards in pay scales. For example, a professional basketball player earns millions of dollars per year, far more than a doctor. Yet a doctor has spent at least 10 years more in education and preparation before he can earn a salary. An executive for a Japanese corporation earns a fraction of an American executive's pay. Yet Japanese corporations currently outperform American corporations in profits, sales, efficiency, and product quality. Surprisingly, the manager of a certain municipal utility in California earns more than the

President of the United States. <u>In short, there is just no rhyme or reason to salaries—there never has been and there never will be. For every job, we can think of another job with equal responsibility and requiring equal education, yet this job has a salary that is far higher; but we can usually find a job with equal responsibilities paying a salary far lower than that of the first two.</u>

C2—Conclusion

In effect, the salary system in any country <u>is like</u> a vast maze. But this is a Kafkaesque maze, a maze without an exit. Normally, when we encounter a maze on paper or even created by evergreen hedges, we expect that after diligent effort we will find a way out that was not the way in. And if a psychologist sends a mouse through a maze, the mouse "imagines" there is a way out, some path that leads to a food pellet or pleasure in the end. Yet in a Kafkaesque maze, this expectation is continually frustrated. For every path the mouse attempts leads to a dead end. Eventually the mouse is forced to return to the beginning. We have seen that the rationale for salaries in our country fits this same dead-end maze pattern. For every earner who sees a "way out," a way to increase wages, the way out leads to higher daily living costs or to an inequity for some other wage earner. If the wage earner seeks an increase based on years of education, there will be low-paid nurses and art historians who will demand more; if the increase is based on responsibility, some voters will point to the relatively low salary of the American president, presumably consumed by responsibility. At every turn in the salary maze the earner is confronted by a dead end. Eventually we are forced to conclude that the maze is not "rational" and that we will all be frustrated mice if we seek to "rationalize" wages.

Notice how the analogy supplies a new structure for the set of details offered in the introduction. While not repeating the thesis word for word, it offers another way of understanding the evidence in the essay's body.

Complement to Introduction

Often you can find a clue to a successful conclusion by rereading your introduction. There you might find some questions that could be answered directly, now that you have developed your thesis with evidence in the body paragraphs. You might find an anecdote that presented a dilemma you can now resolve. You might find an image that has an appropriate counterimage, such as horse/rider or cup/liquid. Each of these approaches **completes** a process begun early in the essay (hence the word **complement**) and, again, provides a reader with a subtle cue, a sense of finish. This essay is in response to Question 1, Chapter 5, page 68:

I3—Introduction

Have you ever encountered an instructor you really appreciated? Have you wondered why that teacher was so effective? What was it about her? Was it simply her knowledge of the subject matter? Obviously, the qualities that make a good instructor are often subtle, not apparent at first. But four qualities are critical: knowledge of the subject, ability to organize material, fairness in responding to diverse student needs, and a sense of humor.

C3-Conclusion

When I took my introduction to psychology course, I encountered Professor Phyllis Young, an instructor I knew I enjoyed. I always wondered what the source of her effectiveness was. Though I understood that she knew behavioral and clinical psychology backwards and forwards, it was only after weeks of analysis that I realized she had the other key qualities of a good instructor: her syllabus provided us with a clear, detailed outline for the course; she treated superior and weak students with the same degree of patience and understanding, and she always had a joke or anecdote I had never heard before in order to illustrate complex issues in psychology.

Notice how the conclusion echoes words and answers questions from the introduction while providing the reader with a proficient restatement of the principal characteristics of a good instructor.

Prediction or Extension

Another technique to create a conclusion offers a prediction based on patterns or ideas developed in your essay. In effect, you offer the reader a natural extension of ideas you have already presented. In using this technique, be careful not to "pull a rabbit out of the hat," — that is, do not assert as a conclusion concepts, generalizations, or ideas for which you have presented *no* evidence in your essay. Be especially sure to avoid concluding with ideas which appear to *contradict* those in the body of your essay.

Here is an example of an effective prediction (we have included the introduction, so that you can see how the prediction follows from the essay's unifying idea):

QUESTION
Examine your life in terms of periods of significant growth or change.

I Led Two Lives

I4 — Introduction

My life can be divided into two distinct periods: the years before and the years after 1980. The difference in me during these two periods has been so radical that the person before 1980 now seems not really me at all — or, to be more honest, I wish it hadn't been. Before 1980, I was alone and confused, tired and disheartened; since 1980, I have become part of a social unit, I have a clear career goal, I'm full of energy, and I am excited. Before 1980 I was a rebellious teenager and, predictably, a single parent with a dead-end job; since 1980 I have become happily married, a parent once again, and now have a clear career goal which is also a vocation, a true "calling."

C4 — Conclusion

Now that I am happily married with a husband closer to my needs and sensitive to my desires, my life has a hopeful shape and a clear direction. I can see myself in five years as an electrical engineer, not just barely scraping by in courses or flunking out, but actually designing complex computer chips. I can see myself as coming home to my children not poor, not enervated, not despairing of the future—but looking forward to its challenge. I also hope that I can raise teenagers using a perceptive sense of the stress, confusion and defeat I suffered when I was one.

NONPROFICIENT CONCLUSIONS

You have probably already guessed some of the characteristics, but you can identify a **nonproficient conclusion** in a number of ways. Perhaps the conclusion is only one sentence—this suggests poor planning and often leaves a reader with only a *pro forma* restatement of the thesis. Perhaps the concluding paragraph consists entirely of essayese, and in no way reworks your thesis or road map.

Or, worst of all, perhaps your conclusion offers assertions for which your essay has not provided a basis. We might call this the **"rabbit-out-of-the-hat"** conclusion. Such a paragraph offers generalizations or refers to undeveloped events or concepts that have no clear tie to the ideas you have developed in the body of your essay—just as a magician shows you a hat that is completely empty, then unexpectedly and inexplicably pulls a rabbit from it. Such surprises are exciting as entertainment, but disconcerting for a reader. Look over the following outline of body paragraph topics and Introduction-I4 (for the essay titled "I Led Two Lives"). Then examine critically the conclusion that follows:

Body Paragraphs
I. Topic A—pre-1980: Independent self, leaving home
II. Topic B—pre-1980: Disheartened self—a dead-end job as a clerk typist, a husband equally ill-adapted to life as I was; a child; a quick divorce
III. Topic C—post-1980: Renewed self—marriage to a lawyer with a secure job, a sense of commitment and affection; second child; no divorce

"Rabbit-out-of-the-hat" Conclusion

There is no question that my life changed radically in 1980. Without the women's movement and my analysis of the war in Vietnam, I would never have been able to make the dramatic change that has propelled me into a career that will compete with the Japanese. I am now happily married, on the road to a better education, and remunerative employment. Most American women have gone through this radical change and are beginning to reap emotional riches beyond their wildest dreams. So the year 1980 was a watershed for all of us; it was not just the election of President Reagan and the reduction in taxes. It was the experience of coming to know ourselves that laid the groundwork for this transformation.

You should notice that though the conclusion touches on *some* issues developed in the body of the essay, it begins to make wild claims and explore topics and subjects not mentioned or evaluated previously. For example, the women's movement, the war in Vietnam, the competition with the Japanese, the extension of the writer's personal experience to *all* American women, and the tie to the election of Reagan are all issues that *seem* brought up out of nowhere. Adding these issues at the end would lead many readers to doubt the logic of the essay and to doubt that it relies on careful thinking substantiated by evidence.

CHECKING YOUR ESSAY

Principal Parts (Introduction, Conclusion, Paragraphs)

After you write your conclusion, you need to spend some time in checking and proofing (for proofing, see Chapter 8). Using the Rules of Thumb, check to see that your essay follows observable main divisions. Do you have an introductory paragraph? Do you have a conclusion? If one of these is missing, insert a short version (remember: your time is limited). Do you have identifiable, proficient paragraphs? If your essay is one long paragraph, simply insert Paragraph symbols (¶) at appropriate places. If you find three or four one-sentence paragraphs in succession, see if they are related and could all be combined into a single, proficient paragraph. If so, use arrows or marginal notations to show the reader that these combine to equal one paragraph. (Though these last-minute changes may be somewhat messy, in the context of a handwritten exam they are usually acceptable and indicate to a reader that you know how to write proficiently.)

Key Words—Unity

Check the question, your thesis statement, and the unifying ideas in paragraphs to make sure you have used **key words** to keep your writing focused. If you have changed terms from your road map to the body paragraphs, you will confuse the reader. Make sure that you are echoing key words to give the reader a sense of unity and continuity. Often, it is necessary simply to change a word or two to make your essay clear. Consider the following question and the writer's thesis, road map, and unifying ideas from body paragraphs:

QUESTION
Discuss a dream you once had and how you view it today.

"Dreams of Dan Rather"

(Thesis) My goal was to become an anchorperson for the evening news, but today I am just a college student majoring in engineering. (Road map) When I was in high school, my heroes were Dan Rather and Barbara Walters; but eventually I realized my talents lay in science and mathematics. Since coming to college, I have embarked on a major in electrical engineering and plan to design newer forms of video recorders and cameras. I now realize that the technology that creates television fascinates far more than the manufactured personalities that feed us our evening news.

Body Par. #1.   I used to watch a lot of T.V.
Body Par. #2.   Gradually I realized that science and mathematics were more appealing to me than journalism and geography.
Body Par. #3.   My current major in electrical engineering is part of my plan to work on the technological end of T.V. and design the components that create the images, not be a manufactured personality that is an image.

Though these isolated elements that reveal the structure of the essay indicate a fairly effective plan, the writer could improve it by echoing key words. Notice that in the thesis the writer uses **goal** rather than the word **dream** from the question. Notice also that the unifying idea for the first body paragraph is much more vague than its parallel version in the road map (watching T.V. versus admiring

Dan Rather and Barbara Walters), nor does it suggest either a **goal** or a **dream.** This writer needs to revise key words in the thesis and topic sentences so that key words from the question are echoed (Try Exercise 7-2, below).

EXERCISE 7-1

1. Write a thesis statement and a conclusion for the following exam topic:

> Discuss a situation in which you had to teach someone something. Then analyze what you learned from this teaching experience.

On a separate sheet of paper, quickly write what you think might be the topics of the body paragraphs for this conclusion. Now, show your conclusion to another student, and ask that student to "guess" the body topics for your essay. Compare your lists of body topics. Is your conclusion a "rabbit out of the hat"?

2. Write a thesis statement and epitome conclusion for the following exam topic:

> Discuss a critical issue confronting us today.

EXERCISE 7-2

Rewrite the thesis and body paragraph topics for "Dreams of Dan Rather" (page 123) so that key words are carefully echoed.

SUMMARY

1. In concluding, avoid using mechanical essayese such as "In conclusion" or "In this essay I have discussed. . . ."
2. Use an effective concluding strategy, such as restating your thesis, offering an epitome example, creating a striking analogy, offering a complement to your introduction or extending your thesis with a prediction.
3. Don't write a "rabbit-out-of-the-hat" conclusion by offering ideas or evidence not developed or suggested by the rest of your essay; moreover, don't contradict your thesis in your conclusion.
4. Leave time to check your essay for the principal parts of introduction, separate body paragraphs, and conclusion.
5. Check for unity by seeing that key words develop clearly from the question asked.

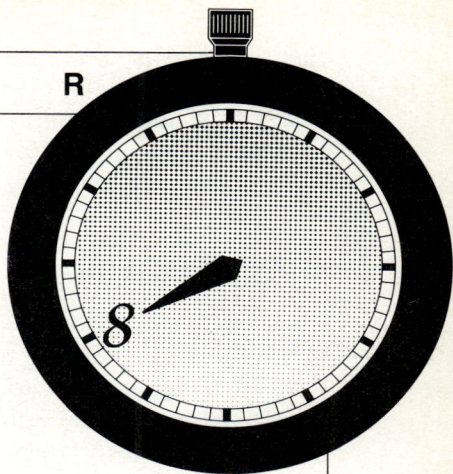

Proofing For Surface Errors

"How 'bout writing a composition for me, for English? . . . Just don't do it *too* good, is all . . . That sonuvabitch Hartzell thinks you're a hot-shot in English, and he knows you're my roommate. So I mean don't stick all the commas and stuff in the right place."

That's something else that gives me a royal pain. I mean if you're good at writing compositions and somebody starts talking about commas.[1]

WHY PROOFREAD?

Most students feel the same way that Holden Caulfield does about commas, proofreading, and other "surface" issues in composition—that they have little to do with really good writing. And most proficient writers would agree. Still, it's necessary to pay *some* attention to these surface details so that the reader can get to the meat of your writing—to see and appreciate your ideas. Too many surface errors fog up your writing and unnecessarily annoy a reader. You might notice that, in the passage quoted above, there are no faults, and it's clear that Holden knows how to use "commas and stuff" correctly.

"But why should I proofread in the first place? After all, I'm just trying to show a reader that I can use ideas and write proficiently. If I made a mistake in spelling or a minor error, the reader would know it was the result of limited time, and that I could go back and fix it if only I had more time." Making such assumptions is risky business.

It *is* true that most intelligent readers will forgive an occasional lapse—especially a mistake that looks like a typographical error. But if you are writing in longhand—as is typical on a proficiency exam and in many other time-pressured situations—you cannot argue that you "hit the wrong key." We know we've all read reputable, published writing in newspapers, magazines, and books that displays an occasional flaw. But how occasional is "occasional"? For each writing task and situation, general expectations and tolerance for errors differ. A 300-page book might contain few errors, but its lengthy publication process may have entailed two years for writing and author revisions, reviews by various editors, plus copyediting and proofreading by professional staff or freelancers during different stages. A daily newspaper of 50 to 100 pages might contain more errors, but many of the articles may have been produced in a span of five to ten hours with very little time for

---

[1]J.D. Salinger's *Catcher in the Rye* (New York: Bantam, 1964), 28. The character Holden Caulfield quoting a friend's comment on his writing.

thorough proofreading. Your writing situation differs from these. Nevertheless, for the reader of your proficiency exam, you need to establish confidence in your own ability to control surface errors and to proofread with relative care. Because a proficient two-and-a-half hour exam yields only about four pages, or 450 to 700 words, an essay with more than 10 errors would probably call attention to itself and raise doubts about your proficiency.

Of course you need to proofread on a proficiency exam because you want to pass. But what are the other reasons? After all, you might think, a reader can understand what I'm saying. Even a sentence fragment or two, several comma splices, and a few spelling errors don't get in the way of *understanding*. But errors like these present temporary barriers and annoyances even to nonprofessional readers (those who are not English teachers or other academics) that lower these readers' estimation of you and your writing. Conversely, error-free writing tends to establish your ideas as those of a trustworthy and proficient writer. This may not be an accurate or logical inference on the part of the reader, but it happens frequently. Proofreading is the task writers like least, but—especially if omitted—it is the aspect of our writing that readers may notice first.

When we have spent two hours writing an exam, or ten hours over a week writing (and rewriting) an essay, we just want to be done with it and leave it alone. We are usually convinced that now it is as good as it will ever be, so we do not want to reread it looking for minor errors. Students, professors, and editors all seem to dislike this task, but it still has to be done.

A few casual errors due to lack of proofreading can distort the reader's impression of your writing—and often of *you* as a person. This is usually unfair, but it is nevertheless the way of the world. Your history professor may spot a few grammatical flaws and some spelling errors and decide to give you a B− rather than a B+. A prospective employer may not give you an interview because your cover letter or resumé contains three sentence fragments and a comma splice. A client or customer may not respond to a report because you misspelled several words in the report. If your writing contains fragments, comma splices, and missing apostrophes, some readers, however unfairly, may make the judgment that you are illiterate. All of these readers are participating in the understandable human game of judging ineffable things by their surfaces—of books by their covers, of college applicants by their SAT scores, of people by their physical appearance. It always seems easier to deal with a vast, variegated phenomenon such as writing by using an objective system—a process of counting or machine scoring. It is so much harder to get at the intrinsic quality—at the great new perception in the book; at the potential in the creative, intuitive student with a low SAT score; at the depth of humanity in someone who doesn't look like Tom Cruise or Kim Basinger.

Readers of proficiency exams counter this tendency by grading "holistically"—not by simply counting errors, but by balancing the effect and overall clarity of the writing against possible oversights in proofreading. Still, you can see that it is to your advantage to reduce errors resulting from proofreading lapses as much as possible.

Proofreading usually follows the writing of the conclusion and checking. It should be the very last activity in composing your exam. Proofreading at earlier stages could be wasteful. As you write, you may decide to omit or revise sentences or even abandon a paragraph after wading half-way through it. If, in these omitted portions, you had to look up spellings, and check punctuation, you wasted your time. Also, worrying about such details while concentrating on ideas can be doubly distracting.

Therefore, save your proofreading time for the very end of the exam and use it efficiently. In fact, that is why you *must* leave time to proof your essay—preferably 20 minutes, but at least 10 minutes in a 2-hour exam.[2] You also need a strategy to make those minutes count—to be an efficient proofreader. Don't just glance casually over your essay; don't check **every** word for misspelling; and don't try to recopy the entire essay assuming that you'll catch an error. Instead, focus on the errors that you have noticed recurring in your writing.

WHAT ARE SURFACE ERRORS?

Some English professors use the term **surface errors,** often casually, to refer to a number of flaws that can be easily detected, that most sophisticated readers agree *are* flaws, and that are distinct from the content or idea structure of the essay. Different text writers and

---

[2]In a non-exam situation, of course you will have more time. But proofreading time won't be there if you don't plan for it. Do not type up a paper in the morning hoping to read it on the way to class. Also, in non-exam situations, you can share proofreading with a friend. Exchange papers and try reading aloud to each other. In any case, don't *ever* turn in a paper—in any class—without proofreading it at least once.

composition teachers call these flaws by different names, but essentially they are errors in spelling, grammar, mechanics, or usage. Some text writers feel that several of these terms are interchangeable with others. In order to be a proficient writer, though, you do not need to understand the categories. You need only master the several types of surface errors that crop up in *your* writing.

Readers differ about the relative importance to attach to particular errors, but repeated errors of any type convince a reader that you cannot control *that* problem; therefore, your writing appears to be not proficient. Also a significant number of different errors, no matter how minor each may seem, lead readers to the same conclusion.

According to a usage panel of 84 professionals in government and business surveyed by Maxine Hairston errors rank in the following descending order of importance:[3]

A. Very serious

   Verb form errors

   Double negatives

   Fragments

   Errors in case

   Fused sentences

   Capitalization errors

   Unnecessary commas

   Subject-verb disagreement

   Adjective for an adverb

B. Serious

   Tense shifts

   Dangling modifiers

   Missing quotation marks; missing commas in a series

---

[3]Maxine Hairston, *Successful Writing*, 2nd ed. (New York: Norton, 1986), 230-233. Adapted from her text.

C. Minor

Faulty use of "whoever"/"whomever"; of "its"/"it's"

Comma splices[4]

Though it is helpful to know of these relative rankings from a particular panel, we have organized our treatment of errors in a different order. Remember also that it would be unwise for you to intentionally ignore *any* type of error—because a critical reader may, for some reason, be obsessed with that particular type.

Nevertheless, you need to compile a personal profile of your own typical errors in order to become a proficient proofreader of your own prose. Look back through graded assignments from your freshman composition class and from other courses that required expository writing (term papers, essay exams, etc.). If you have already taken a proficiency exam and can get a trained reader to review it with you, go over it together, looking for surface errors. On a separate sheet of paper, isolate each surface error by type, then tabulate the results to find the most frequent types of errors you make. Learn how to quickly locate and correct these in your own proofreading.

In the rest of this chapter we discuss the major types of surface errors. Our order and our choices of errors depend on *similar* categories of errors: for example, related errors in identifying and punctuating independent clauses or sentences are linked together. Our categories do not attempt to rank errors in order of relative severity. The errors we treat here do not exhaust all possible types, but are those typical of proficiency exams with failing grades. Consult the endpapers of this text for a table of abbreviations for errors. In the following discussion, we have printed abbreviations in **bold.**

---

[4]Many readers, especially composition instructors, consider the comma splice a very serious error, *not* a minor one. You should certainly understand how to avoid a comma splice; consult your instructor as to your campus' or state's view of the relative severity of this error.

Hairston's professional panel felt some errors in pronoun/antecedent agreement do not matter; but we feel many readers object to these, so you should pay attention to them—and that is why we discuss them in this chapter.

Sentence Limits and Interior Punctuation

Surface errors under this heading consist of fragments **(frag)**, comma splices **(cs)**, fused sentences **(fs)** or run-on sentences **(ros)**; or errors in the use of the comma **(ce)** and semicolon **(se)**. (You can find a fuller treatment of these issues in Chapters 9 and 10).

frag—Make sure each sentence you write contains both main subject and main verb. Be especially careful when giving examples. Check carefully sentences with "-ing" verbs to make sure these sentences contain main or helping verbs; check carefully sentences that begin with subordinating words **(after, although, as, as if, as though, because, before, if, in order that, since, so that, that, though, unless, until, when, wherever, whether, while)** to make sure there is an independent clause (see Chapter 9, pages 152 to 157) as well as a dependent (or subordinate) clause (see Chapter 9, pages 157 to 159).

cs—Check for commas; circle them lightly in pencil. Be sure you have not used a comma when you should be using a period or semicolon. If the word groups on both sides of a comma could stand alone as sentences, use a semicolon or a period (see Chapter 9, pages 161–163).

fs/ros—Check long sentence blocks. Do they contain *two* (or more) independent clauses **(IC)?** If they do, use periods or semicolons to separate the clauses. Often, fused sentences are a result of writing in a hurry and not realizing you have neglected to punctuate the end of one sentence before going on to the next (see Chapter 9, pages 163 to 165).

ce—put a comma after introductory material and after each item in a series; surround parenthetical material with commas—use the "suitcase" test (see Chapter 10, pages 168 to 172); use commas to link independent clauses joined by coordinating conjunctions (one of the "*FANBOYS*": **for, and, nor, but, or, yet, so**).

se—look for semicolons and circle them. Make sure each word group before and after a semicolon is a sentence (independent clause). To test, ask yourself if a period could be used instead of the semicolon (see chapter 10, pages 172 to 175).[5]

EXERCISE 8-1

In the sentences below indicate if there is a fragment, comma splice, or run-on sentence error. Then correct each error. The corrections you make will be in punctuation only. DO NOT OMIT ANY WORDS to correct an error; however, you may ADD WORDS to correct an error. Some sentences may be correct.

1. In just a minute. I'm going to lose patience with this task.

2. Mark lost his part-time job he couldn't continue in school.

3. Gunner is a college senior, his sister runs a beauty shop.

4. While in Chicago, Elisa visited the Sears Tower. The tallest building in the world.

5. Our employee incentive plan is simplicity itself, make one mistake and you're fired!

6. The card catalog is an important library research tool every student should know how to use it.

7. Most assignments are given to add to a student's knowledge; they are not supposed to be just "busy work."

---

[5]Of course, a semicolon may be used between items in a series that themselves contain commas—you are unlikely to use a semicolon this way *in error* if you understand the semicolon rules that well. Therefore, we ignore the series rule in giving you advice for proofreading.

8. I believe teaching is an overcrowded profession, many experts agree

with me.

9. Kim worked all night that's why she's sleeping now.

10. David bought a pound of cherries. And ate them in one hour.

11. Whenever Eden is late, her reason is that her watch has lost time.

12. Rod didn't work hard last month his boss didn't promote him.

EXERCISE 8-2

Examine the following paragraphs quickly (pretend you are proofreading your own work; give yourself a limited time, such as 10 minutes). Identify and correct surface errors such as fragments, comma splices, and semicolon, or other punctuation errors.

One professor I had was particularly annoying. Especially because of his habit of giving unannounced quizzes on difficult homework. For example five pop quizzes in one month. He would assign, say, 60 pages of reading in modern physics, then the next class day he would give us a 20 question quiz on the difficult parts of the homework, such as, equations for the theory of relativity. Or Shrodinger's wave equations.

But he was not the only professor with a distinctive behavior that interfered with my learning. Not at all. A history professor expected us to memorize the dates of every significant event in the last hundred years; even events I considered insignificant and I stayed up all night trying to memorize those dates. We had to memorize dates; such as the following; when World War I began; when it ended; when the two atomic bombs were dropped on Japan; when the Watergate break-in occurred; and many other seemingly obscure dates. And needless to say. I failed.

Worst of all was my art instructor, I could never understand what she wanted. Because she would rarely offer any instructions or guidelines. She would simply move from table to table. Occasionally offering a word of advice, suggestion or encouragement. When we did line drawings she put on her Sony walkman, when we were working with construction paper she talked only with her friends among the other students, but when we finally got to clay she did offer some advice to me. But, I still got a B in the class.

Subject-Verb Agreement

Agreement errors occur when two related words should both be singular or plural and are not. The most common agreement errors occur when a subject is singular and its verb is plural (or vice versa) or when a pronoun is plural and its antecedent is singular. (For definitions and more information on subject and verb, see Chapter 9.) Standard English grammar requires that subjects and verbs **agree** in "number"; that is, singular subjects require singular verbs; plural subjects require plural verbs. Here are several examples of these subject-verb agreement faults. In the parenthesis following the sentence, we have identified the subject (S) and the verb (V):

F1. There is many voters who favor the death penalty. (S = voters; V = is)

F2. The beginning of philosophical inquiries are typically difficult. (S = beginning; V = are)

F3. An amoeba, just like bacteria or a virus, are difficult to locate, even under a microscope. (S = amoeba, V = are)

You might notice that in F2 and F3 the faults occur because the subject is separated from the verb by an "of" clause or a parenthetical expression. The writer mistakes an intervening noun for the subject of the verb. These faults can be eliminated if you remember the following rules: **Rule 1:** The *object* of a preposition can never be the *subject* of a sentence. "Of" is a preposition. **Rule 2:** Intervening parenthetical phrases—those beginning with "like," "as," etc.—are not the subject and do not affect or add to the number of the subject. For example, the subject in F2 is beginning, not inquiries. A compound subject (such as two singular nouns joined by "and") is plural. Once you identify the true subject for the verb, it is usually easy to correct the agreement problem:

C1. There are many voters who favor the death penalty.

C2. The beginning of a philosophical inquiry is typically difficult.

C3. An amoeba, just like bacteria or a virus, is difficult to locate, even under a microscope.

If you know you have this particular problem, you should develop a proofreading strategy to correct it. You might locate all sentences where the subject is separated from the verb by a clause or a phrase, or simply use a light pencil line to connect suspect subjects with verbs, then check to see that they agree in number.

Often using the oral test will help. Say only the subject-verb combination out loud. Ask yourself if that "sounds right." For example, in the sentence "The basket of apples weigh six pounds," say "The basket . . . weigh." That should sound awkward to you.

EXERCISE 8-3

Look for subject-verb agreement errors in the following sentences. Circle the subject and underline the verb; then correct errors by making the subject agree with the verb, or by restructuring the sentence. Some sentences may be correct.

1. Swimming around boats is difficult.

2. If one of the boats are moving very quickly, even skillful swimmers can encounter breathing, location, and strength problems.

3. My reality and my education is very important to me.

4. When I began my education, I saw that books of any kind is more exciting than I had once supposed.

5. There is differences of opinion among authorities who are involved in the study of criminal behavior.

6. Several courses required for Mark's major is not being offered this semester.

7. The ceiling, as well as the walls, are freshly painted.

8. Annie's favorite fruit is bananas.

9. Each of the tools needs repairing.

10. A completely different set of rules has been made for this game.

11. Neither the tigers nor the lion was on display at the zoo.

12. Fred and Ethel plays cards with Lucy and Ricky.

Pronoun-Antecedent Agreement

Typically, pronoun agreement errors involve use of one of the following words:

anyone	each one
everyone	nobody
everybody	no one
anybody	every
each	a person

Though as we write these words, we may feel that we are dealing with a large group, a universe, or something plural, the grammatical status of these words is that they are *singular*. Therefore *singular* pronouns (**his, her, he, she,** or **one**) must be used in referring to any of these words; or the sentence can be restructured so that the pronoun is unnecessary. Here are some examples of faults in pronoun agreement:

F1. Every student must take general education classes as well as classes in <u>their</u> major.

F2. But each is destined to be disappointed in <u>their</u> career choice.

F3. Although everybody eventually finds an apartment, <u>their</u> initial hunt is maddening.

F4. A person must do <u>their</u> job competently or they will be fired.

F5. Each guest thanked the hostess before <u>they</u> left.

Each of these examples raises a slightly different problem, but each can be corrected by making sure that pronoun and **antecedent** (the noun the pronoun refers to) agree in number:

C1. Every student must take general education classes as well as classes in <u>her</u> major.

C2. But each is destined to be disappointed in <u>his</u> career choice.

C3. Although everybody eventually finds an apartment, the initial hunt for one is maddening.

C4. A person must do a job competently or risk being fired.

C5. Each guest thanked the hostess before leaving. (Or, Each guest thanked the hostess before <u>he or she</u> left.)

EXERCISE 8-4

Correct the errors in pronoun agreement in the following sentences. Some sentences may be correct.

1. No one wanted their picture taken.

2. The electric company and the water service raised its rates this year.

3. The company moved their office to San Francisco.

4. If an accused person needs a lawyer, they can get them from the Public Defender's office.

5. All the girls must pay her deposits before leaving on her trip.

6. Neither the Joneses nor Mr. Smith enjoyed their trip.

7. Both the Joneses and Mr. Smith enjoyed his trip.

8. A student should be proud when they get an "A."

9. Nobody understood where they went wrong on the quiz.

10. The committee cast their vote.

Shifts in Pronoun Use; You

When you begin to use one pronoun in your essay to refer to a particular person or idea, you should continue to use the same pronoun throughout. This is a subtle form of agreement and also prevents you from unnecessarily confusing the reader. For example, if you begin your essay writing about "students" in the third person, you should not suddenly shift to "you" (the second person) to refer to the same group:

> Emergency room patients are often subjected to ineffi-
> cient procedures. These patients bear the brunt of their own
> traumatic injuries, of medical professionals under great
> stress and often with little sleep, and of a bureaucracy
> obsessed with paper forms and payment. After entering the
> emergency room, you are asked to fill out about 15 forms.
> Then, four hours later, with incessant pain in your arm, a
> nurse leads you to a small cubicle and leaves you alone.

The writer begins this paragraph referring to "emergency room patients" in the third person, then shifts abruptly to "you," the second person. But the reader may never have been in an emergency room. In general, particularly when you are writing under pressure for a large, general audience, it is best to avoid "you." **Do not use "you" to refer to the reader, to yourself, or to people in general.** Instead, use the third person ("he," "she," "it," "the patient") or the first person ("I"). Of course, "you" is appropriate in a "how-to-do-it" essay (explaining to the reader how to perform a task) or in a letter. You have probably noticed that this text uses "you" because we really are addressing you as students directly and expect you to employ some of the strategies we suggest.

Suppose you find that you typically have pronoun errors. In proofing, search for pronouns, and test them for *consistency* (does this pronoun refer to the same thing/person as its last use in an adjacent phrase, clause, or sentence?), *agreement* (is its number the same as the thing/person it refers to?), and *shifts* (have I switched unnecessarily to "you"?).

Apostrophes

Most students know how to use apostrophes correctly in contractions such as **don't, won't, can't.**[6] Some proficiency exam readers

---

[6]It might help you understand the apostrophe by realizing that even apostrophes for possessives result from omission or contraction. In the early stage of our language, known as Anglo-Saxon or Old English, nouns varied in form—or were declined—for each grammatical position taken in the sentence. There was a special form for the possessive—or genitive—usually involving **-is** or **-es**. For example, Modern English **ship** was originally **scip**; its genitive or possessive form was **scipes**. Over the years, the pronunciation of the **e** diminished and vanished, and the possessive form began to be pronounced **ship s.** The apostrophe evolved to indicate the omitted letter: **ship's.**

feel that using contractions is inappropriate; other readers are not troubled by them at all. In general, contractions lend a sense of informality to your writing, and—occasionally—a colloquial tone. If these seem inappropriate for your subject, or if instructions for the exam explicitly warn against contractions, don't use them. As you can see by our last sentence, we do *not* avoid contractions; but you should check with your instructor to determine attitudes at your college or university.

The type of apostrophe use that gives students the most trouble is the apostrophe showing possession. In order to use an apostrophe to show possession, remember two simple rules:

1. If the *base form* of the possessor *does not* end in -s, add 's to show possession. (The base form is the form the word would take in the sentence if you were not trying to show possession.)

    EXAMPLES:

Base Form	Possessive Form
dog	dog's
girl	girl's
men	men's
bicycle	bicycle's
Joe	Joe's
Smith	Smith's
crux	crux's

2. If the *base form* of the possessor *ends* in -s, add only the ' to show possession.[7]

Base Form	Possessive form
Zeus	Zeus'
dogs	dogs'
Smiths	Smiths'
tuxes	tuxes'
bicycles	bicycles'

---

[7]Some editors, grammarians, and writers prefer to add -'s (instead of simply the ' alone) after certain nouns in the singular ending in -s: **Zeus's wife Hera; William James's famous book,** *Psychology;* **happiness's worst nightmare.** But this extra -s is *not,* in our opinion, required: our advice is to add -s if you would pronounce it; otherwise, just follow the two rules above—it is easier.

Here are some examples of correct use of the apostrophe in a variety of possessives:

C1. A dog's bite is worse than its bark.
C2. The girl's purse was, for some reason, found in the men's room.
C3. "Nately's whore's kid sister's room" represents a famous use of the apostrophe in Joseph Heller's *Catch-22*.
C4. If Leda cannot put on Zeus' power, perhaps she can acquire his knowledge.
C5. When we went to the Smiths'[8], we were unable to locate the street address.

In proofing, you can typically check for missing apostrophes by looking for a certain grammatical structure within a sentence: a noun ending in -s, followed by another noun. Here are a few examples:

1. boys bikes
2. Georges house
3. Zeus sister
4. womens liberation

Each of these constructions requires an apostrophe for the first word; a quick analysis will show whether the apostrophe should precede the -s or follow it. For example:

1. The possessive word is *boys*. What is the base form? If one boy owns all bikes, the base form is *boy* (it does not end in s, so we add 's to form the possessive), and the proper form for the expression is *boy's bikes*. If the bikes are owned by two or more *boys*, the base form is *boys* (it ends in s, so we add ' to form the possessive; and the proper form for the expression is *boys' bikes*.
2. The possessive word is *Georges*. In English, there is only one possible base form: *George*. Therefore, to indicate that *George* lives in or owns the house, the proper form is *George's* house.

---

[8]This form of the possessive is usually misunderstood or misused. Here "the Smiths'" is an abbreviation for the house or apartment where the Smiths reside. Note that the base form is "Smiths" (a plural: it is a whole family of Smiths).

3. *Zeus* is the possessive word. There is only one Zeus in Greek mythology. Therefore, the base form is *Zeus*. To make *Zeus* possessive, we need only add an apostrophe: *Zeus' sister*.
4. *Womens* is the possessive word. The base form of *womens* is *women* ("women" is already plural). To make *women* possessive, we add *'s* and the proper form is *women's liberation*.

EXERCISE 8-5

Check the following sentences and add apostrophes in appropriate places. Some sentences may be correct.

1. A students first duty is to his education.

2. The difference between psychology and philosophy lies more in ones preference than in ones spelling.

3. The man-of-wars naval architecture was effective in its time, but a distinct disability in the following age.

4. Authors houses don't look any different than anyone elses house.

5. One of the great films of the French *nouveau vague* was François Truffaut's *Shoot the Piano Player*.

6. Every American schoolchild is taught about Columbus discovery of America in 1492.

7. The Ellerbees home was a raucous place—full of dirty diapers, unpaid bills, broken furniture, and an undiminished sense of humor.

Verb Forms and Verb Tense Shifts

Most college writers already know the principal parts of verbs:

> I <u>see</u> now (Present); two years ago I <u>saw</u> (Past); I <u>had seen</u> many like this (Past Perfect).

> You <u>exaggerate</u>; two years ago you <u>exaggerated</u>; in fact, you <u>have exaggerated</u> many times in the past (Present Perfect).

If you have any difficulty with these verb *forms*, you should study them carefully and check those that you are uncertain about in a dictionary. Do this checking when you reach the **proofing stage** of your writing; before that, you may eliminate the particular verb in revision, so looking it up in the dictionary would waste time.

Often writers who have no trouble forming the principal parts of a verb occasionally make errors in the third person singular in the present tense:

> Because Todd, as a runner, <u>anticipates</u> the rest of the race, he <u>paces</u> himself.

Even though it may seem inconsistent with the ways plurals are generally formed for English verbs, the sign of the third person *singular*, present tense, is an <u>s</u> added at the end. If you have a problem with this feature, in your proofing, check sentences with "he," "she," or "it": link subject to verb, then make sure the verb has the proper ending.

Even if you know how to **form** verbs properly, you may still have a problem with verb **tense shifts.** In general, make sure you have chosen an appropriate time or tense—and that you stay in that tense while describing events that occurred at the same time. For example, if the events described happened in the past, consistently use past tense. Do not arbitrarily shift to the present:

F1.

When I <u>was</u> 12, I first <u>learned</u> I <u>had</u> epilepsy. It <u>was</u> one of the most disturbing events of my life. It <u>caused</u> a great trauma for the doctor explaining it to me, for my parents, and of course for me. I <u>go</u> into the waiting room wondering what <u>has been going</u> on in my head. My doctor <u>looked</u> at the brain scan and <u>began</u> to speak. He <u>says</u>, "Jim, this <u>is</u> very hard for me to say to you; but you really <u>shouldn't be</u> unduly alarmed. You <u>have</u> epilepsy; but epilepsy <u>can be controlled</u> with medication."

This writer begins in the past tense, switches to the present tense, then shifts to the past tense for the doctor's entrance, and then back to the present tense for what the doctor says. Yet all these verbs refer to the same incident 12 years ago; it would be more proficient, and less confusing for a reader, to place all these verbs in the past. (You should note that the direct quotation uses present tense verbs. This is proficient because conversations, quoted directly, take place in the present.) Here is a version using more appropriate tense choices:

C1.

> When I <u>was</u> 12, I first <u>learned</u> I <u>had</u> epilepsy. It <u>was</u> one of the most disturbing events of my life. It <u>caused</u> a great trauma for the doctor explaining it to me, for my parents, and of course for me. I <u>went</u> into the waiting room wondering what <u>had been going</u> on in my head. My doctor <u>looked</u> at the brain scan and <u>began</u> to speak. He <u>said</u>, "Jim, this <u>is</u> very hard for me to say to you; but you really <u>shouldn't be</u> unduly alarmed. You <u>have</u> epilepsy; but epilepsy <u>can be controlled</u> with medication."

EXERCISE 8-6

Rewrite the following sentences to make verb tense, or time shown in the verbs, consistent.

1. By the time Willa Cather became editor of *McClure's Magazine* in New York, she lives in Virginia, Nebraska, and Pennsylvania. She will be strongly influenced by her years in Pittsburgh.

2. Many teachers say that there are four kinds of writing. One kind was narration; another would be description; a third type is exposition; and last there will be argumentation.

3. I get lonely when I am tired, when I spent too much time with strangers, or when my emotions will get churned up.

4. At first, the princess refused to marry the handsome prince because he wears polka-dot ties. Later, however, she realizes his clothes didn't matter as long as he was a kind person.

Doubles

By **doubles,** we mean word pairs that sound alike or look similar on the page and are often confused. You may have encountered them before as "homonyms" (literally, "same names"). Make a *short* list of the ones that cause *you* trouble, then look for these in proofing.

it's/its—*it's* means "it is"; *its* is the possessive form of *it*. If what you've written cannot be replaced by "it is," use "its" without the apostrophe. **(This is one of the few exceptions to the two rules we have given you for using apostrophes to show possession.)**

were/where—*were* is a verb, the past tense of the infinitive form "to be"; *where* is an adverb designating place.

then/than—*then* is an adverb of time referring to the past; *than* is a conjunction used in comparisons. Therefore, *then* often occurs at the beginning of a sentence, *than* in the middle of one.

weather/whether—*weather* is the ever-changing temperature, atmosphere and external conditions that make up our world and often affect our psyches; *whether* is a conjunction used to introduce alternate possibilities.

you're/your—*you're* means "you are"; *your* is a possessive adjective for the second person. If what you've written can't be replaced by "you are," use *your*.

they're/their/there (technically a "triple")—*they're* means "they are"; *their* is a possessive adjective for the third person plural; *there* is a place slightly further away, as distinguished from *here*.

two/too/to (another triple)—*two* is the "letter" version of the number 2 (try replacing what you've written with "2" as an initial test); *too* is an intensifying adverb meaning that there is more than enough of something, or *too* can mean the same as *also*; *to* is either a preposition (usually quickly followed by a noun) or introduces an infinitive (that is, it is quickly followed by a verb).

are/our—*are* is a verb, the present plural form of "to be"; *our* is a possessive adjective for the first person plural "we."

knew/new—*knew* is the past tense of the verb "to know"; *new* is an adjective for something that is recent, as opposed to "old." If you are in doubt, you might test by substituting "old"; if the sentence becomes nonsensical, the version you want is *knew*.

affect/effect—*affect* is a verb meaning "to have an influence on"; *effect* is a noun meaning a result or change.[9]

accept/except—*accept* is a verb meaning "to allow or acquiesce in"; *except* is a verb meaning "to exclude or omit."

know/now—*know* is a verb meaning "understand or have knowledge"; *now* is an adverb meaning "immediately."

Myself

You simply need to be aware that this word is often misused. If you use it, make sure that you have used the word "I" in the same sentence; if not, change "myself" to "I" or "me." "Myself" is a reflexive pronoun, a word used when action turns from the subject back to the subject; thus it can only be used when the subject of its clause is "I."

F1.   She hurt myself when she broke off our relationship.

C2.   I hurt myself while shaving this morning.

---

[9]Though the uses are much more rare, two other meanings attach to this double. There is also, in the jargon of psychology, the word *affect*, a noun meaning a particular emotion or its behavioral display. Further, the word *effect* can be a verb meaning "to bring about." Notice that when *effect* is used as a verb the causal relationship is much more emphatic, less in doubt than with *affect* as a verb.

The first sentence displays a grammatical error and should be revised:

C1.   She hurt me when she broke off our relationship.

EXERCISE 8-7

Check the following sentences and correct errors in use of doubles or "myself."

1. Its not always important whether your rich or not.

2. His criticism didn't effect me very much, aside from my immediate desire to commit suicide.

3. When the grades came out, it was a great pleasure for myself to see the A beside my name.

4. Joe's interest in computer programming was far greater then his interest in the opposite sex.

5. There problem was that they could not understand weather to perform the experiment first or apply for the funds first.

6. After eating to much ice cream, are inclination was to go home and take "infinity" naps.

7. I was fixing the car myself, but I new that I would have to call the mechanic in two hours and pay an outrageous bill.

8. The film's producers now say that they can't bring it in under budget without shooting the star or reducing his salary.

9. The affect of that symphony on myself was greater than I knew.

10. Despite the dog wagging it's tail, Grace was afraid of being attacked and

bitten.

Spelling

Virtually all writers need to proofread for spelling. However, each person's method will (and should) vary. First, you shouldn't rely on the few minutes of proofreading time to correct a multitude of spelling errors. If you frequently misspell, you need to pay special attention to this problem and try to correct it through tutoring and study. You should make a list of frequently misspelled words. Keep a small spiral notebook (pocket size) in which you write each word, spelled correctly, at the top of a single page; then copy the same word down to the bottom of the page. Add new words to the notebook as you discover others you misspell. Check through the notebook occasionally, and review it carefully on the day before the exam.

As you compose your draft, don't worry about spelling. When you come to the proofing stage, check a few suspicious words—don't waste a great deal of time trying to make sure your spelling is perfect; other surface errors are far more important. Nevertheless, if you have used words from the question itself, you should take special care to make sure that these are spelled correctly (as they are in the question).

SUMMARY

1. Allow time for proofing.
2. Make your own personal list of typical surface errors to check for. From the summary items a–g, select those items that apply to you.
   a. Check for sentence units and punctuation: fragments, comma splices, semicolon use.
   b. Check for errors in subject/verb and pronoun/antecedent agreement.

c. Check for faulty pronouns.
d. Check for missing apostrophes.
e. Check for verb form and tense shifts.
f. Check for double problems and misuse of "myself."
g. Check for occasional spelling errors.

The Sentence: An Independent Unit of Thought

THE SIMPLE SENTENCE OR INDEPENDENT CLAUSE
THE FRAGMENT
THE DEPENDENT CLAUSE
THE PHRASE
COMMON SENTENCE PROBLEMS
  Comma Splice Errors
  Fused Sentences

In Chapter 4 you reviewed paragraph construction to better understand the process of organizing and supporting your main ideas. You learned that a proficient paragraph is a group of related thoughts controlled by a unifying idea and that readers rely on this paragraph structure to make sense of your ideas. Writing proficiently is also important at the sentence level. Writing clear, accurate sentences is actually your first step to developing coherent paragraphs and essays: we consider a sentence a *basic unit of thought*; writers combine individual thoughts to support main ideas in paragraphs.

You have undoubtedly already learned some basic principles about sentence construction in previous English classes. You are also quite aware of the mechanical signs: a capital letter is the beginning and a period the end signal for a sentence. These mechanical signs are a guide readers use to determine when one thought stops and another begins. Just as a paragraph indentation helps readers see the structure of your main ideas, sentence signals identifying sentence limits help readers to understand your individual thoughts.

But mechanics alone do not make a word group a sentence. This chapter will review sentence construction, focusing on the difference between a whole thought, or sentence, and a fragment. What constitutes a sentence? Why are fragments confusing and considered nonproficient? What's the difference between an independent and a dependent clause, and how is each used? Why are comma splice sentences or fused sentences troublesome for readers? These questions relate to problems writers may face as they formulate their ideas into sentences. Understanding the fundamentals of sentence construction will help you express your thoughts more clearly and proficiently.

THE SIMPLE SENTENCE OR INDEPENDENT CLAUSE

We compose sentences using three different word groups: **independent clauses (IC), dependent clauses (DC)** and **phrases (P).** Each word group has a unique function, and we often combine word groups to express thoughts. However, *only the independent clause can stand alone as a sentence.*

Perhaps you remember (from another English class) a sentence being defined as "a complete thought." That definition, once thought accurate, is now considered vague and evasive or ambiguous because, in some sense, both a paragraph and an essay express a complete thought as well. A more specific definition of a sentence identifies it by looking for grammatical units. A simple sentence is a group of related words that contains *one main subject* and *one main verb.* (Often a simple sentence may contain details that tell more about the subject or the verb, such as adjectives, prepositional phrases, or objects.) The subject and verb *function as a unit* to form the sentence's **grammatical core**. In this core, the verb expresses an action or state of being, and in the active voice, the subject tells who or what is performing that action. This grammatical core gives a reader the basic information needed to understand the thought *by itself*. For example, note the core parts in the following simple sentences:

> A strange looking man lurked at the playground's edge.
>   subject   verb   prepositional phrase

> The bewildered student pondered the difficult test question.
>   subject   verb   object

> Usually Paula is very enthusiastic.
>   subject   verb   predicate adjective

These groups of related words are sentences because each has a grammatical core and can stand alone—a reader can fully comprehend the writer's message in each unit of thought and can move on to the next unit or sentence without confusion.

The grammatical name for this simple sentence structure is **independent clause.** In a **simple sentence,** the entire word group is called an *independent clause* because the thought can be understood *independently* of any other word group. In a **complex sentence,** we use the term *independent clause* to designate a *main thought* when combining a simple sentence with other word groups. In addition, we can combine two or more independent clauses to form a **compound sentence.**

EXERCISE 9-1

Identify the grammatical core (main subject and verb) in each of the following simple sentences. Remember that the core parts function as a unit; whatever you identify as the subject must perform the action or be subject to the state of being expressed in the main verb.

1. A penny saved is a penny earned.
2. Swimming is Cass's favorite activity.
3. Tom asked you not to say that!
4. Hidden on the hill stood the deserted mansion.
5. Isabel's stubborn computer refused to obey her command.
6. A map showing the state's eleven air basins is on page 3.
7. Elizabeth! Say something about your father's tie!

THE FRAGMENT

Earlier we said that a capital letter at the beginning of a word group and a period at the end signaled a sentence. When readers see these signs, they expect the word group to make sense or be understandable *by itself*. However, what happens when the sentence signs are there, but the sentence structure is missing? Confusion![1] Typically only independent clauses—word groups that contain a grammatical core and can stand alone—can begin with a capital letter and end with a period. When you put these sentence signals with any other word group, you are misleading and frustrating the reader.

A word group that is not an independent clause—but is still punctuated as a sentence—is called a **fragment.** A fragment is like a picture puzzle with pieces missing. You have an idea of what the picture is, but because pieces are missing, you don't know **exactly** what it is. A fragment is a group of words punctuated as if it were a sentence, but either the main subject or the verb—or both—have been left out. With one or both of these core pieces of information missing, a fragment presents only part of the thought, requiring the reader to fill in what is missing.

Fragments are nonproficient because they confuse readers, who can't always determine exactly what omitted information the writer had in mind: readers can't see the whole picture. A fragment is a serious error which writers should avoid in *all* writing situations—exams, term papers, class assignments, business or even personal letters. When you *read* a fragment, you can sense something is wrong with the statement, but you don't always know what. Sometimes you'll reread the statement, thinking you've overlooked some information. Then you discover your confusion is caused by a careless writer, who gave you the sentence signals but not all the sentence information. Now carefully read the following statements.

S1. The man, being of sound mind.
S2. Made in the U.S.A.
S3. Clean that mess right now!
S4. Starting with our senses.
S5. As Courtney laughed at me.

Even though each statement begins with a capital letter and ends with a period, do you feel all these statements can stand alone, or do you sense that something is missing from the thoughts? Many times you can tell if a statement is a sentence or a fragment by simply saying it out loud; this is called the "oral test." When you

---

[1]We hope you noticed that this is a fragment. Is it justified? Does it interfere with your ability to read the paragraph?

actually say the words, often you can "hear" if the statement is complete or if it needs more information. For example, say statement 1 out loud. Does it sound complete or do you feel you need more details to complete this thought? If you are also saying to yourself "What about the man being of sound mind?" you know the statement is a fragment—it has no main verb to tell what the man *is doing*. All of these statements *except #3* are fragments. Statement 3 is a sentence; it has an *implied subject*—"you"—a verb—"clean"—and an object—"that mess." But the others have core parts missing. Statement 1, as we said, has no main verb; statement 2 has no subject; statement 4 contains only part of a verb (a "verbal" or participle) and no subject; and statement 5—even though it has both the subject and verb—is a fragment because it begins with the word "as" which makes it a *dependent clause*, and dependent clauses cannot express the *main* subject and verb. (Dependent clauses are explained in the next section of this chapter.)

Why do writers write fragments? Can't they tell that something is missing from the word group? Not always.[2] Often fragments are left over pieces of thoughts or afterthoughts—information that actually belongs with the sentence directly before or directly after the fragment. But instead of including the fragmented thought with a main thought, the writer separates the fragmented thought and punctuates it as if it could stand alone. Here are some examples:

F1. Not only was I angry. But also frustrated.
F2. Marita swam ten laps every day. *Though it was hard for her.* She passed the lifeguard test.
F3. *Although Dominic really likes camping.* He'd rather stay in a motel.

In the *writer's mind*, these constructions probably make sense. But readers view fragments differently. Remember, readers expect word groups that begin with capital letters and end with periods to make sense alone. Readers cannot always determine which main thought, or sentence, the fragment is meant to be a part of. For instance, in F2, the fragment though it was hard for her could

---

[2]This looks like another fragment, but some grammarians consider a direct answer to an immediately preceding question to contain the implicit grammatical structure of an entire sentence.

logically go in either the sentence before *or* the sentence after it. How is a reader to know where to attach it?

There are two ways to correct fragments: add the fragment to an adjacent sentence, or add the missing core part (subject, verb, or both) to the fragment to make it a sentence. Here are corrections for the fragments in the previous example:

C1.

Not only was I angry. But also *I was* frustrated.

(subject and verb added to fragment)

C2.

Marita swam ten laps every day though it was hard for her. She passed the lifeguard test.

(fragment added to sentence before)

OR

Marita swam ten laps every day. Though it was hard for her, she passed the lifeguard test.

(fragment added to sentence following)

C3.

Although Dominic really likes camping, he'd rather stay in a motel.

(fragment added to sentence following)

Although fragments can confuse readers and you should avoid them in your essays, occasionally you may choose to write a fragment for a specific reason: to startle a reader, to single out a thought, to create a sense of tension or abruptness. An occasional fragment for effect can enhance your writing, *as long as readers understand your mistake is for a purpose.* Notice how effective the fragments are in the following examples.

F1.

She was pure California. Tall. Blonde. Tan.

F2.

The stereo sounded bad. Really bad.

F3.

I told him I wanted it fixed today. Not tomorrow. Not next week. Today.

F4.

New York cheesecake. Baby Ruth bars. Fettucini Alfredo. These were the sacrifices Lisa had to make to lose that 50 pounds.

The fragments in these sentences are **not** mistakes. The writers used them purposely to single out and emphasize certain parts of the sentences. Unlike the fragments in preceding examples, these fragments actually add to the expression, making the statements more meaningful. For example, notice how the sense changes and the effect is lost when the fragments are corrected.

NF1. She was tall, blonde, tan, and pure California.
NF2. The stereo sounded really bad.
NF3. I told him I wanted it fixed today. I did not want it fixed tomorrow or next week. I wanted it fixed today.
NF4. Lisa had to sacrifice New York cheesecake, Baby Ruth bars, and Fettucini Alfredo in order to lose that 50 pounds.

Proficient writers know how and when to use fragments for effect, but understand that generally they should avoid fragments.

EXERCISE 9-2

Underline the fragments in the following groups of sentences. Then rewrite each group, correcting the fragments by either adding the fragment to the sentence before or after it, or adding the missing parts (subject and/or verb) to the fragment to make it a sentence.

1. It was a frustrating morning. Yelling at the kids to get ready on time. Then we rushed out the door. Barely made it to school on time.

2. It didn't just rain; it poured. In buckets. Flooded the streets, the gutters, the driveways. We thought it would never stop.

3. I'm taking an 8:00 a.m. class this semester. Although I hate getting up early. The discipline is good for me.

4. Some people enjoy living in remote spots. Whereas others enjoy living in the city. Despite all the traffic.

5. Whenever I look at Vicky. I get a strange feeling. As if I have known her in a past life.

THE DEPENDENT CLAUSE

The **dependent clause** is a group of related words that contains a subject and a verb, but is considered a fragment because the reader needs more information to understand it: a dependent clause *depends* upon other information in the sentence for full meaning. Though in a dependent clause the subject and verb aid a reader in understanding, this clause cannot stand alone and make sense. (The verb in a dependent clause **is not** the *main verb* of a sentence, nor is the subject the *main subject*.) Dependent clauses express information that is additional or accessory to the main thought (independent clause) of a sentence. Therefore, dependent clauses *must* be combined with independent clauses. Note how the following sentences combine a dependent clause **(DC)** with an independent clause **(IC)** to express the thoughts more thoroughly. The dependent clauses are underlined.

> S1. A strange man lurked on the playground's edge <u>as if he belonged there.</u>

S2. <u>Because he had not studied</u>, the student was bewildered by the difficult test question.

S3. <u>Although Paula seems rather bored today</u>, usually she is very enthusiastic.

You could try the "oral test" on these sentences by saying <u>only the underlined portions</u> out loud. You will hear that just the dependent clauses do not provide a complete thought; you can't make sense of them *alone*.

You can often spot a dependent clause (and avoid punctuating it as if it were a sentence) by the *first word of the clause*; dependent clauses generally begin with **dependent words:**

after*	although	as, as though, as if
because	before	even though
if	in order to	in order that
once‡	provided that	since
so that	than	that
though	unless	until
what†	when	whenever
where	whereas	wherever
whether	which†	while
who/whom†	whoever/whomever	whose

*SOMETIMES USED AS A PREPOSITION
†CAN BE USED TO BEGIN A QUESTION
‡ONLY WHEN USED TO MEAN *WHEN* OR *IF*

Note the dependent clauses (dependent words underlined) in the following examples:

S1. <u>While</u> Nolan was at the store, a thief broke into his house.
     DC   IC

S2. My major is English <u>whereas</u> Josephine's major is math.
           IC   DC

S3. Frank had soup and salad <u>before</u> he had the main course.
       IC   DC

S4. <u>Unless</u> you passed the test, you will fail the course.
     DC   IC

S5. I told him <u>that</u> I absolutely refused to marry him.
     IC   DC

If we eliminated the *independent clauses* in the example sentences, the dependent clauses would not make sense standing alone:

DC1. While Nolan was at the store.
DC2. Whereas Josephine's major is math.
DC3. Before he had the main course.
DC4. Unless you passed the test.
DC5. That I absolutely refused to marry him.

But if we eliminate the *dependent word,* the dependent clauses would become simple sentences:

SS1. Nolan was at the store.
SS2. Josephine's major is math.
SS3. He had the main course.
SS4. You passed the test.
SS5. I absolutely refused to marry him.

Remember, dependent words introduce dependent clauses, and dependent clauses should not be punctuated as sentences. Dependent clauses are *fragments;* they cannot stand alone and make sense.

EXERCISE 9-3

Identify the dependent clauses in the following sentences by circling the dependent words and underlining the entire dependent word group.

1. Whenever I feel depressed, I watch a Mel Brooks movie which always cheers me up.

2. Even though the chocolate mousse tasted like chalk, Arianna ate every bit of it because she didn't want to disappoint the chef who had worked so hard to prepare it.

3. As if having the leading part in the play were a great hardship to her, Marie vowed that she would never act again once the play was over.

4. I enjoy listening to a variety of music, whereas my sister Fran has listened to nothing but the Beatles since she was two years old.

THE PHRASE

Another kind of fragment is a **phrase.** A phrase is simply a *group of related words.* Though these words make some sense together, they do not constitute a sentence; a phrase has neither a subject nor a verb. You are probably most familiar with the **prepositional phrase**—a group of related words that begins with a preposition, such as *around the corner, in the house, beyond the trees, above the rooftops, under the table, at home.* Notice how these groups of words make some sense to you, but each forms only a part of a thought. For example, *to the Italian restaurant* is a prepositional phrase in the sentence "Anita went *to the Italian restaurant.*" The words in this phrase relate to each other and the phrase gives the reader more information about where the subject of the sentence—*Anita*—went. But by itself, the phrase does not make sense. Or in the following example, note how an introductory phrase gives the reader more information about the subject ("the knight").

> <u>Sword in hand</u>, the valiant knight rode off to slay the dragon.

The phrase *sword in hand* is interesting, but accessory to the main idea expressed in the independent clause: "The valiant knight rode off to slay the dragon." Like a dependent clause, a phrase should not be punctuated as if it were a sentence.

EXERCISE 9-4

1. Identify the underlined word groups as either a PHRASE (P), DEPEN-DENT CLAUSE (DC), or INDEPENDENT CLAUSE (IC). Refer to your list of *dependent words* if you are unsure.

_____   **a.** Chris wanted to organize a softball game, <u>but no one would cooperate.</u>

_____   **b.** Joel really likes movies, so he goes once a week <u>even though he can't afford to go that often.</u>

_____   **c.** Snow skiing requires special equipment, <u>such as skis, boots, poles and insulated clothing.</u>

_____   **d.** <u>As Elisa read Randall's farewell letter</u>, tears streamed down her cheeks.

_____   **e.** <u>After using a computer just once</u>, Steven vowed never to handwrite a paper again!

_____ **f.** In the 1960s wearing "love beads" was popular <u>whereas in the 1970s people preferred to wear gold chains</u>.

_____ **g.** A major earthquake hit <u>San Francisco</u> during the third game of the 1989 World Series.

_____ **h.** Today cars are built for economy <u>and not for speed</u>.

2. Identify the following word groups as either phrase, dependent clause or sentence. Then add information to the phrases and dependent clauses to make them sentences.

_____ **a.** Although Valerie didn't want to go.

_____ **b.** Until the storm finally broke.

_____ **c.** The old man standing in the alley.

_____ **d.** Once Paul finishes the painting.

_____ **e.** Give the prize to whomever claims it first.

_____ **f.** For example, six essays and a research paper.

_____ **g.** Jogging through the park is a daily activity for Linda.

_____ **h.** Whereas Ken prefers long hikes.

OTHER COMMON SENTENCE PROBLEMS

Besides the fragment, two significant sentence-level errors to avoid are the **comma splice** and the **fused sentence.** Both are punctuation errors which cause readers confusion. You are giving the reader the wrong punctuation signal (comma splice) or no punctuation signal at all (fused sentence). Proficient writers are careful to punctuate according to established conventions.

Comma Splice

A comma splice is an error that occurs when a writer puts a comma between _two independent clauses_ instead of separating them with a period or joining them with a semicolon or a coordinating conjunction. The result is two independent thoughts or two separate sentences spliced together as if they were one. Why is this punctuation confusing or misleading to a reader? Because an independent clause (sentence) expresses only _one main thought._ Readers interpret a comma as a _slight pause within that main thought;_ they expect to continue reading the _same thought_ after that pause until the writer ends the independent clause with a period. Putting just a pause at the end of one independent clause and then continuing with a new independent clause fails to make the proper distinction between the two thoughts. This punctuation is ambiguous: the thoughts are separate, yet the punctuation suggests they are one. The following sentences are examples of comma splices. Notice that the word groups before and after the commas are independent clauses.

CS1. Steve carefully opened the door, no one was in the dimly-lit room.
CS2. We had steak for dinner on Tuesday, on Thursday Patric will arrive from London.
CS3. The restaurant menu was extensive, fish was a specialty.
CS4. It snowed three feet last night, the power went off.

One way to correct comma splices in the example sentences is to replace each comma with a period:

S1. Steve carefully opened the door⊙ No one was in the dimly-lit room.
S2. We had steak for dinner on Tuesday⊙ On Thursday Patric will arrive from London.
S3. The restaurant menu was extensive⊙ Fish was a specialty.
S4. It snowed three feet last night⊙ The power went off.

As you read the sample sentences, though, you may notice that there is a connection between the two independent ideas expressed in each sentence (which is often the case in comma splices). However, a comma is not an appropriate mark to either separate the two independent ideas *or join them*. If you want to put two (or more) independent clauses in one sentence, you must link them with either a *semicolon* or a *comma and a conjunction*.

JS1. Steve carefully opened the door⦂ no one was in the dimly-lit room.

or

Steve carefully opened the door⊙ but no one was in the dimly-lit room.
JS2. We had steak for dinner on Tuesday⦂ on Thursday Patric will arrive from London

or

We had steak for dinner on Tuesday⊙ and on Thursday Patric will arrive from London.

JS3. The restaurant menu was extensive⊙ fish was a specialty.

or

The restaurant menu was extensive⊙ <u>yet</u> fish was a
specialty.

JS4. It snowed three feet last night⊙ the power went off.

or

It snowed three feet last night⊙ <u>so</u> the power went off.

(Note: writers sometimes like to link closely related independent clauses with transitional words such as *thus, therefore, however, consequently,* and so forth. Though these words help to connect independent thoughts, they *do not* function like conjunctions to actually *join* the thoughts. The two independent clauses must first be joined with a semicolon, which is then followed by the transitional word and the next independent clause. Here is an example:

Steve carefully opened the door⊙ <u>however,</u> no one was
in the dimly-lit room.

Also note that the transitional word is followed by a comma. See Chapter 6 for more information about using transitions.)

Fused Sentence

A **fused sentence** occurs when a writer neglects to put any punctuation at all at the end of one independent clause (sentence) and simply continues with the next. This error, also known as a **run-on sentence,** is a problem for readers because they have no indication of where the writer wants one thought to end and another to begin: the sentence signals are missing. The writer has *fused* two or more independent clauses by failing to separate them with appropriate punctuation. Therefore, to make any sense of fused sentences, readers must guess where the writer intended to punctuate. And even if they don't have to guess, they still have to reread the fused thoughts and supply punctuation. Here are some examples of fused sentences. Read them carefully; you will have to determine where punctuation should have gone.

FS1. The thesis of this essay is obvious all people are responsible for their own experiences.

FS2. Time sheets are due on Friday the accountant will be in to
pick them up.

FS3. Sometimes I am just amazed why people can't learn from their mistakes is beyond me.

FS4. Anyone can play at tennis however learning to play skillfully takes years of practice.

Did you notice that you first read the sentences through from capital letter to period; then you noticed some confusion in meaning, so you reread, looking for the problem? You may have had to read the sentences a third time to determine exactly what the writer was trying to say and where punctuation should have gone. The second example sentence is particularly ambiguous—were time sheets due on Friday, or will the accountant be in on Friday? The third example sentence causes confusion because you *think* you are reading *one* idea until you get to the word "is." Then in rereading, you discover that a period or semicolon should have gone after the word "amazed." The fourth example illustrates how a transitional word is not enough to connect the two independent clauses; punctuation is still needed at the end of the first independent clause (after the word "tennis") to avoid fusing it with the second. In all four examples, the fused sentence error interrupts your concentration on the writer's message; instead, you become concerned with correcting the writer's error.

Proficient writers understand the confusion and frustration that fused sentences cause and avoid making this serious sentence error. They are careful to either end each independent thought with appropriate terminal punctuation (period, exclamation point, or question mark) before going on to the next, or join two (or more) independent thoughts with a semicolon or a conjunction. Here are the corrected versions of the example sentences. Notice how much easier they are to understand.

S1. The thesis of this essay is obvious⊙ all people are responsible for their own experiences.

S2. Time sheets are due⊙ <u>and</u> on Friday the accountant will be in to pick them up.

or

Time sheets are due on Friday⊙ The accountant will be in to pick them up.

S3. Sometimes I am just amazed⊙ Why people can't learn from their mistakes is beyond me.

S4. Anyone can play at tennis⊙ however, learning to play skillfully takes years of practice.

Comma splices and fused sentences are common errors in writing. They often occur because writers are in a hurry to get out all their ideas and are not concentrating on punctuating properly or because they fail to proofread when they are done writing. You as a writer know the boundaries of your thoughts, but when your writing has comma splices or fused sentences, you either improperly indicate or have forgotten to indicate those important boundaries to your reader. That is why proofreading your papers for mechanical errors such as comma splices and fused sentences is important and must be a part of your writing strategy.

EXERCISE 9-5

Identify the independent clauses in the following paragraph. Then correct the comma splices and fused sentences.

As an artist, Mary Cassatt was unique in several ways. First, she was a woman, most women of her time did not aspire to careers in the arts in fact it was so unusual for a woman to succeed in the arts that many female writers of the time, such as the Brontës, wrote under male pen names just to get their work published. Cassatt did not let her gender stop her from developing her talent as an artist, she was, in fact, the only really important female artist and the only significant American painter to become an expatriate in France she was also the only American to be accepted into the central French Impressionist group. Another aspect of Cassatt's life that was different than most artists of her time was that she came from a wealthy family, her father was a wealthy banker, she and her family lived elegantly in Paris or in the French countryside as she pursued her career as an artist and later an art collector she had no financial worries.

SUMMARY

1. The simplest sentence is grammatically designated as an independent clause and consists of a subject and a verb.

2. A group of words beginning with a capital and ending with a period which doesn't contain an independent clause is a fragment. Fragments confuse readers because they are not complete thoughts: they have core information missing (main subject, main verb, or both).

3. Occasionally, fragments are effective in expository prose. But you should check most sentences carefully to see that they have both a main subject and a main verb.

4. Word groups that sometimes look like sentences but are not are dependent clauses (beginning with dependent words) and phrases.

5. Comma splices and fused sentences are two serious sentence-level errors that cause readers confusion. Proficient writers are careful to avoid both of these errors.

6. Proofreading for errors in sentence limits—fragments, comma splices, fused sentences—is important.

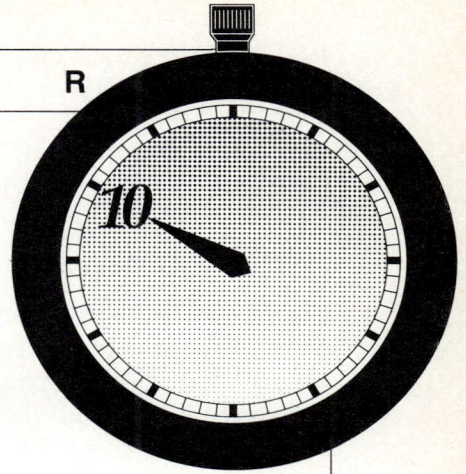

Punctuating Sentences Proficiently

USING COMMAS
USING SEMICOLONS
USING COLONS
USING DASHES

In Chapter 9, you learned that the independent clause **(IC)** is the basic unit of the sentence and consists of subject and a verb. Without these elements, you have no sentence: in effect, if there is no independent clause, there is a sentence fragment. As you write more complex sentences, it is often effective to add material in various forms to the independent clause. In order to write proficiently, you now need to review punctuation to add this material effectively to the basic sentence unit.

If all you have is a simple independent clause, you need no punctuation other than a period:

The president signed the treaty.
Subject   Verb   Object

Virtually all forms of **interior** sentence punctuation (comma, semicolon, colon, dash) help you to add material effectively to the independent clause without confusing a reader.

USING COMMAS

Let's begin with the **comma** (,). Though there are many ways to discuss the use of the comma, we will consider four main comma uses. Essentially, the comma is a slight pause allowing the reader to see easily how additions mesh with the basic sentence unit.

C1. Use a comma to connect two *independent clauses* joined by a *coordinating conjunction*. The coordinating conjunctions are these: **for**, **and**, **nor**, **but**, **or**, **yet**, and **so**. You can remember them with an acronym some composition instructors created by using the first letters of these: FANBOYS. Here are several examples of commas used with coordinating conjunctions:

The road was dark(,) and we were very frightened.

Communism has usually been thought to originate with Karl Marx(,) but many cultural analysts trace its history to early Christian communities.

Typewriters seem to produce typographical errors(,) so we prefer to use computers with word-processing programs and spell-checkers.

You should notice that a comma before a coordinating conjunction alerts the reader to a second major thought unit (independent clause).[1]

---

[1]Because independent clauses beginning with coordinating conjunctions are truly independent, they may also be punctuated as individual sentences:

The road was dark. And we were very frightened.

Communism has usually been thought to originate with Karl Marx. But many cultural analysts trace its history to early Christian communities.

Here the difference between comma and period may seem slight; the period tends to emphasize the separation—and particularly the contrast—more. In addition, semicolons may also be used to separate independent clauses linked with coordinating conjunctions, particularly when one of the clauses contains a comma. See the discussion of semicolons in the following pages.

Some readers may think that beginning sentences with conjunctions such as *and* or *but* should not be encouraged. We believe that using them occasionally for emphasis creates effective stylistic variety.

C2. Use a comma to separate an introductory element from the independent clause. Introductory elements may be single words, phrases, or dependent clauses (introductory elements in the examples below are *in italics*):

> *Condescendingly,* the wine steward asked whether we preferred steak with white wine.

> *In short,* he was tried and hanged.

> *Even if the budget deficit is absorbed in the coming years,* America will suffer a strategic wound in its economy for decades.

> *To avoid penalty,* fees must be paid. [Notice how, as in so many cases, the comma here avoids confusion and prevents the reader from having to reread the sentence.]

You should see that the comma in each case immediately precedes the subject of the independent clause, thus subconsciously aiding the reader in seeing the center—or main thought—of the sentence.

C3. Use commas to separate parenthetical material from the rest of the sentence. Unless the material appears at the very beginning or very end of the sentence, this guideline requires **two** commas. Many nonproficient punctuations occur because writers begin to separate parenthetical material from the sentence by using one comma, but fail to insert the **second** comma. This confuses the reader, who is often forced to reread the sentence:

Not Proficient

Professors⊙ those arbiters of grades hurt students with their power.

Proficient

Professors⊙ those arbiters of grades⊙ hurt students with their power. [Note how inserting the second comma after **grades** avoids temporary misunderstanding, as well as enlightening a reader puzzled as to the reason for the comma after **Professors.**]

Parenthetical material is that which is not essential to the sentence core. You can test to see if the material is parenthetical using the "suitcase test"—surround the material with commas and "lift" it out of the sentence. Does the sentence still make sense? Is its core meaning left about the same? Then the material you lifted is truly parenthetical and *requires* the two commas to separate it from the rest of the sentence. If you were speaking (or especially, acting on a stage), the parenthetical material would be uttered as an aside. Study the following examples (parenthetical material has been underlined):

Dogs, often regarded as "man's best friends," are descended from wolves. [Notice if you remove the parenthetical element, **often regarded as "man's best friends,"** you are left with an independent clause, the core of the sentence: **Dogs are descended from wolves.** As the core meaning of the sentence is unchanged, the parenthetical element passes the suitcase test.]

A final distribution, reflecting property sales and other investment proceeds, will be made in December. [Notice that the phrase **reflecting property sales and other investment proceeds** simply explains the nature of the distributions, but does not change the meaning or core of the sentence.]

He loved her; she reminded him, however, of a very sick Airedale. [Occasionally even single words, particularly transitional adverbs, are also parenthetical. Notice that in the sentence above, **however** is used differently than in the following, without commas: "However intensely we may love someone for the first six months, that intensity eventually diminishes." In this sentence, **however** modifies "intensely" and is *not* a conjunction.][2]

C3a. Some potentially parenthetical elements require special attention—these are relative clauses which begin with **who, which,** or **that.** Clauses like these either define or restrict the meaning of the nouns they follow and refer to. Here the decision to use commas requires that you first examine the *meaning* of the sentence. Consider the following sentence and the element in italics:

V1. All humans *who take money for sexual favors* are prostitutes.

Punctuated as above, without commas, it is simply a conventional definition of prostitutes. But suppose we make the underlined element parenthetical:

V2. All humans, who take money for sexual favors, are prostitutes.

---

[2]Besides "however," some other transitional adverbs are the following: accordingly, also, anyhow, besides, consequently, furthermore, hence, incidentally, indeed, instead, likewise, meanwhile, moreover, nevertheless, otherwise, still, therefore, thus, undoubtedly. Often these adverbs begin clauses, so that each is surrounded by a semicolon (or period) and a comma—rather than two commas.

Using the suitcase test, this sentence makes a radical statement with which few would agree—that all human beings are essentially prostitutes and that no one engages in sexual intercourse except for financial gain. Inserting the commas makes the underlined element parenthetical—non-essential to the core of the sentence. The meaning of V2 is quite different from that of the earlier version (V1). The lesson to be learned here is to read sentences carefully when deciding whether **who, which,** or **that** clauses are parenthetical and require commas.

C4. Use commas to separate items in a series. Series are quite often extensions of some element in the independent clause (subject series, verb series, object series) and the commas aid the reader in seeing the series as a unit. Though advice differs on this issue, it is probably easiest for you to put a comma before *and* when it precedes the final item in the series.

> Mazda, Honda, and Toyota have all recently inaugurated luxury lines of autos to compete with BMW and Mercedes. [Commas link the three nouns that form the subject.]
>
> In *Seven Chances* Buster Keaton skips, jumps, hops, stumbles, and ultimately evades an avalanche of giant stones. [Commas link the five verbs in series.]

C4a. Use commas to separate coordinate adjectives in series. You can test to see if two or more adjectives are coordinate by substituting an **and** for the comma:

> The stark, bulbous nose of the figure in the painting drew attention unlike any other characteristic. [We could write "stark and bulbous nose," so the comma here is appropriate.]
>
> Archibald was a dark circus bear with the demeanor and neuroses of a human being. [Here we could not write "a dark and circus bear," so there is no comma.]

C5. *Don't* use a comma to connect independent clauses that lack coordinating conjunctions, as in the following pattern:

IC, IC

For that reason, the following sentence is *not* punctuated proficiently:

> We were not aware of the difficulty they had encountered reaching us by telephone, our answering machine needed new batteries.

This results in a comma splice (see Chapter 8 for more information on comma splices); the comma should be replaced with a period or semicolon:

Proficient

> We were not aware of the difficulty they had encountered reaching us by telephone; our answering machine needed new batteries.

USING SEMICOLONS

The **semicolon** (;), as its visual image suggests, is midway between a comma and a period—a more emphatic pause than a comma, a less emphatic pause than a period. Mastering the two essential uses of the semicolon often subtly indicates to readers that you can control a variety of sentence forms as well as punctuate proficiently. It is sad and somewhat startling, but many intelligent college graduates remain uncertain about how to use the semicolon. Often they even avoid the semicolon entirely, thus depriving their writing of greater diversity and clarity—because the semicolon is one of the major types of punctuation. Though it is possible to go through your writing life without ever employing a semicolon, you can often improve the readability of your writing and make complex sentences comprehensible by strategic placement of semicolons.

S1. Use a semicolon to link *related* independent clauses. In theory, it is acceptable to use a semicolon between any two sentences. But the primary reason to use it is to show that the two sentences are more closely related than a mere period would suggest. Often sentences are related because one answers a problem posed in the other, or because both share the same style, or because the second reveals the effect of which the first is the cause, or because the second clause explains a key idea in the first. It might help you to remember this rule by using this abbreviation:

> IC; IC.

Here are several examples:

> The Old Testament and the New Testament are related; Judaism and Christianity are related.

This was Robert Kennedy's most serious problem⊙ he wanted to run for president against the war in Vietnam, but McCarthy had already been there before him.

Seize the day⊙ you are unlikely to find the next one quite as desirable.

Of course these sentence pairs could have been punctuated with periods:

The Old Testament and the New Testament are related. Judaism and Christianity are related.

This was Robert Kennedy's most serious problem. He wanted to run for president against the war in Vietnam, but McCarthy had already been there before him.

Seize the day. You are unlikely to find the next one quite as desirable.

Though periods here are acceptable, using semicolons—particularly when these sentences occur in the midst of paragraphs—aids the reader in seeing the structure of your thought. The occasional semicolon is a subtle cue (like the indentation for a paragraph) that shows a pair of thoughts with more links than those around them, that shows a micro-organization to your thinking as well as a macro-organization.

S2. Use a semicolon to separate units of equal grammatical rank, particularly when the sentence already contains commas. For example, independent clauses are of equal grammatical rank, so this guideline, in effect, also includes S1. An independent clause and a dependent clause are of unequal rank, so a semicolon would be inappropriate to separate these two (see S3 below). Items in a series are of equal grammatical rank. Therefore, a typical use for this guideline is in a series where many of the items in the series already contain commas. (Hint: This means that there will be at least two semicolons; also you *must* have a semicolon before the "and" that introduces the final item on the list.)

I went to the store and bought apples, oranges, pears⊙ toilet paper, paper towels, lunch bags⊙ and <1> charcoal briquets and <2> lighter fluid. [The semicolons help the reader see that the shopping list falls into three related groups: fruits, paper products, barbecue materials. Each group contains interior commas, thus necessitating a "heavier" unit of punctuation to separate groups. Note that **and** <1> introduces the third category in the main series, while **and** <2> only connects the two shopping items in that category.]

Our reading list for the summer consisted of a novel, Kesey's *One Flew Over the Cuckoo's Nest*; a book of poems, Stevens' *Harmonium*; and a play, Glaspell's *Trifles*. [You might notice that the commas above separate parenthetical explanations for each item in the series. Therefore, one of the reasons for using a semicolon to replace a comma is the confusing number of ways in which a comma can be used in a sentence. If you used only commas here, it might seem that there were six items in the list, rather than three.]

S3. There are **no other uses for semicolons.** If you are contemplating using a semicolon and it does not fit guidelines S1 or S2, you should not use it. Therefore, do not use a semicolon to introduce a list; do not use a semicolon to separate a dependent clause from an independent clause because these are not of equal grammatical rank (**DC; IC** not proficient). Here are several errors—nonproficient uses of the semicolon:

Not Proficient

Life takes many forms; plants, animals, viruses, bacteria, a magazine. [This semicolon won't work because it separates an IC from a phrase—these are not of equal rank. Use a colon or a dash.]

Proficient

Life takes many forms: plants, animals, viruses, bacteria, a magazine.

or

Life takes many forms—plants, animals, viruses, bacteria, a magazine.

Not Proficient

When any activity is examined in detail and with skill; it becomes more exciting and intriguing. [This semicolon won't work because it separates a DC from an IC—these are not of equal rank. Use a comma.]

space between mountains and ocean. It does have Death Valley and it is just this side of Mexico. But it is dominated by the visual media by the trivialization of value associated with Hollywood and television. Its culture can be defined in a single phrase second-rate.

SUMMARY

C1. Use a comma between independent clauses joined with a coordinating conjunction.

C2. Use a comma after an introductory element.

C3. Use commas to separate a parenthetical element.

C4. Use commas to separate items in a series.

C5. *Don't* use a comma to connect independent clauses that lack a coordinating conjunction. This results in a *comma splice*.

S1. Use a semicolon to join independent clauses.

S2. Use a semicolon to separate units of equal rank.

S3. There are no other uses for the semicolon.

CL1. Use a colon to introduce a word, phrase, or independent clause.

D1. Use a dash to interrupt an independent clause.

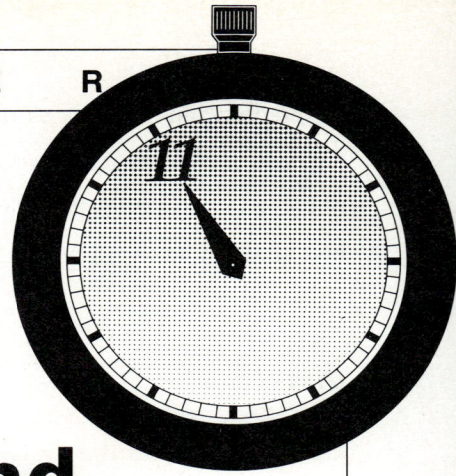

Words— Choosing and Pruning

BLAND, GENERAL WORDS
DODO VERBS
CLICHÉS
REDUCING WORDINESS
  Avoid Essayese
  Avoid Unnecessary Hedges
  Remove Placeholder Words
  Seek the Hidden Verb
  Reduce Repetitive Phrases to Single Words
  Replace Roundabout Expressions with Concise Alternatives

People are interested in a variety of things. Some things are good for them. Others are bad. When people get interested in these things, they often go to great lengths to get what they want. If these people make the right choice, then things are good. But other people do different things in other areas. That has to be bad. But it is interesting because many people make bad choices in their lives. Throughout my life bad things and good things have made life interesting.

Is this paragraph proficient? It has a unifying idea (apparently). It develops that idea. It has no surface errors—no flaws in punctuation, grammar, or spelling. Yet if you found this paragraph obnoxious, boring, or disappointing, you are like many readers. The difficulty in this paragraph derives from two sources—which are, in a way, the same source. It lacks concrete detail, and its vocabulary is unvaried, bland, even confusing to some readers.

Very few of you currently write paragraphs this weak (in fact, it is not a *student* sample at all, but one *we* constructed to exaggerate a tendency we see in some nonproficient essays). Still, many of you probably recognize in the paragraph some elements characteristic of your own writing—some deficiencies you have feared for years. You may notice, for example, the irritating repetition of words like **thing, interesting,** and **people.** You probably label this tendency in your own writing as a "weak vocabulary."

But the problem is not that your vocabulary is truly weak; your problem is that you don't take advantage of your personal lexicon—the practical dictionary in your mind. To say this another way, by the time you have reached the junior year in college, you have encountered, you understand, and you remember many more words than you ever use in your writing. You may imagine that in order to combat this perceived deficiency, you need a thesaurus, so that you can sprinkle your essays with words like **terpsichore, sesquipedalian,** or **tetragrammaton.** Nothing could be further from the truth! All you really need to do, particularly on a proficiency exam, is to change a few key words—often in the proofreading stage. To do this, focus on and change these kinds of words: vague, bland words; "dodo" verbs; and bland phrases—often called clichés. This chapter will help you to do that.

Of course, as you practice these techniques as part of proofing, you will also begin to use them in your drafting stages, and the level of your writing in general will become more proficient. You will begin to ask yourself immediately as you write whether "thing" or "people" is the best, clearest, most specific choice for what you mean.

BLAND, GENERAL WORDS

Some words, by their very popularity, prove poor choices. This group of words changes every generation and probably reveals hidden tendencies in our society. But what concerns us here is the overuse of this group of words, why the words are inadequate, and how you might replace them. Ironically, it is the popularity of these words that is killing them. Often, the more use a term gets, the less meaning and power it offers to a reader—and the more its meaning becomes confused, vague, and imprecise.

Take, for example, the most widely used and most "dangerous" word in this group—the word **thing:**

> The things in my room are constantly getting in my way.

> In an Introduction to Psychology course, a student learns many things that prove useful in a career as a clinical psychologist.

> My divorced mother's most annoying characteristic is this thing she has for the tennis pro at the club.

> Many things in human life are difficult to understand or endure.

None of these uses of the word **thing** is particularly unclear or notably difficult, yet each writer could have found a far better, more specific word as a substitute. In these examples, the word **thing** can refer to inanimate objects, to abstract ideas, to unexpressed or indefinable or censored emotions, to virtually any essence that is not alive. It is not in itself wrong to use the word **thing** (or its derivatives **something, anything, everything**); but notice how much clearer the above examples become with appropriate substitutions:

> The books, papers, and furniture in my room are constantly getting in my way.

> In an Introduction to Psychology course, a student encounters many theories and techniques that prove useful in a career as a clinical psychologist.

> My divorced mother's most annoying characteristic is her infatuation with the tennis pro at the club.

> Many traumas of human life are typical, but difficult to understand or endure.

No single one of these substitutes is the *only* proper one; no single one is always the *best* choice. But simply forcing yourself to think of substitutes for **thing** inevitably makes your writing sharper and clearer.

When we are talking, we often use the word "thing" to refer to some subject or matter because we are in a hurry, can't think of a better word, or are focused on another issue. But in writing, there is more time and need to be precise, and the effect of finding appropriate substitutes for "thing" is that readers see us as better educated, clearer, less given to sloppy thinking and messy expression—that is, we present ourselves as proficient writers.

Just as **thing** is often an overgeneral word choice, the same is true for the word **people** (or the typical phrase **many people**):

> Many people in college don't know why they are there.

> People are fearful of the crime wave currently sweeping the streets, and politicians take this fear into account.

Though this word is sometimes appropriate or useful, a proficient writer usually finds that searching for alternatives presents a clearer idea. It is effective to use **people** when the broad spectrum of humanity taken as a species or a behavioral group is intended; otherwise, seek a more specific alternative:

> Many students don't know why they enroll in college.

> American voters are fearful of the crime wave currently sweeping the streets, and politicians take this fear into account in planning their campaigns.

You will notice that seeking alternatives often yields a reshaping of other phrases in the sentence, helping you to develop an implicit idea.

Let's examine one final example of a bland, general word—**interesting.** Many of us use this word in conversation to avoid making a commitment, judgment or decision:

> The painting I saw at the art show was interesting.

> Education is an interesting process.

> The interaction among the four vacationers on the year-long voyage was quite interesting.

Yet proficient writing does make a commitment or offer a judgment. Though these sample sentences are not worthless, they avoid saying very much. In fact they avoid the processes of judgment, evaluation, and analysis which are what most students learn in college. Though **interesting** may be an appropriate word at a cocktail party or other social situation to avoid embarrassment, it is worth considering replacing during the proofing process in writing:

> The painting I saw at the art show was obscene and puzzling.

> Education is a paradoxical process in which one pays good money often to receive negative self-evaluations.

> The interaction among the four vacationers on the year-long voyage provided a case study of personality disintegration.

The point for all of these word substitutions is that there is no *one* right answer, no *one* right replacement. The process of seeking a replacement itself, in general, refines the sentence—making it clearer, more proficient. In addition to words like **thing, people,** or **interesting,** consider the following words as also suspect, dangerous, potentially overused, and vague:

different—This modifier is easy to use, hard to define. Different from what? How different? Do you mean unusual? Eccentric? Unique? Disturbing? Complicated?

bad—This modifier is an easy classifier of human beings, events, artistic works, and other negative experiences that most of us begin to use in speech as early as the second grade. In effect, it is a catch-all negative that we often use when speaking. "Bad" tells us very little about the writer's judgment of an event, person, moral, issue. Do you mean evil? Disappointing? Demoralizing? Depressing? Financially disastrous?

life—(particularly in phrases such as "throughout my life" or "in my life"). When you are writing a personal essay, there is a great tendency to add prepositional phrases containing "life." But doesn't this go without saying? Isn't it obvious? Consider: "I have learned from all my experiences throughout my entire life." Suppose we drop the phrase "throughout my entire life." Is the meaning of the sentence unclear? Who else's life would have your experiences? When else would you have these experiences except "in life"? In death? If you know a great deal about the experiences of someone "in death," you are a very special individual indeed.

varied, various—This modifier is often a substitute for "different." The word may sound sophisticated at first, but what have you really told the reader? Snowflakes are varied; so are people; even automobiles, mass-manufactured at 300,000 a year are "various." Try to be more specific—if you have "varied" friends, perhaps you have "friends with radically opposed values or hobbies." This word might work if it is followed by sentences with concrete examples of the variety you wish to point to.

very—This modifier of adjectives is a catch-all intensifier, a step above "pretty" ("pretty good"): "very good," "very interesting," "very important." Reduce your use of "very." Often, you can improve your sentences by removing "very" entirely and leaving the word it modifies to stand all by itself, or by replacing it with an adjective that already contains the connotations of "very":
very happy = happy or ecstatic
very funny = funny, humorous, or hilarious

terrible, awful, tremendous, wonderful—These are colloquial adjectives that have minimal power when you are speaking, and virtually none when you are writing. Don't rely on them alone to make your writing vivid.

EXERCISE 11-1

In the following sentences or passages, identify bland, unnecessarily vague words, and substitute more specific words. Often you will need to replace one word with several, or to create a context for or meaning in the sentence that is not there in the original. You might also wish to add a few sentences of concrete detail to amplify or clarify whatever word you substitute.

1. Many things interest me.

2. People are always trying to cope with difficult problems in life.

3. Various bad things happen to Karen whenever she enters a car.

4. Many people find the prospect of an evening with a beautiful woman quite interesting.

5. People experience many areas of life as they grow.

6. Different problems are encountered in education.

7. Einstein discovered a tremendous difference when he contemplated the nature of time and space.

8. My education gave me a wonderful gift.

9. Parents tend to become awfully attached to varied things in their children.

10. Throughout my entire life I have experienced difficulty.

DODO VERBS

A second strategy for vocabulary reform in proofing (or in the original drafting stages) lies in refining verbs. Verbs are generally considered the key words in a sentence, the words that, if effectively chosen, can make the sentence come alive. Verbs generally are located in the middle of sentences both geographically and as part of the meaning structure—the verbs carry the action (or idea) from subject to object.

Certain verbs, however, can weaken writing through overuse or because of blandness or because they are mere **"placeholders"** in the sentence. In the sense that these verbs **deaden** the sentence, we may refer to them as **dodo verbs**. The main dodo verbs are forms of **to be (is, are, were, was), to have, to make,** and **to do:**

> It <u>is</u> a great feeling when I find a job on the job placement board.

> I <u>had</u> to wait half a year to receive a response from the Social Security Administration.

> <u>Make</u> a commitment <u>to</u> <u>be</u> a better writer.

> Most people want <u>to</u> <u>do</u> good for others.

> I <u>have</u> always <u>taken</u> pleasure in <u>making</u> up comedy routines.

> Lawyers can <u>do</u> anything they want.

> Inflation <u>is</u> a direct result of high employment.

You might notice that these dodo verbs creep into expressions that have a colloquial flavor, that seem to come directly from speech.

Because dodo verbs often echo the vagueness, casualness, or sloppiness of speech, you can improve your writing by eliminating or replacing many of them. Often another word (usually a noun) in the sentence contains the kernel of a more proficient verb. We call this **seeking the hidden verb.** For example, look at the following sentence:

> **A decision** was made to **not** give **subsidies to students.**
>
> **(Hidden verbs underlined; dodo verbs** not in bold.)

The two nouns **decision** and **subsidies** contain "hidden" verb forms. In effect, the dodo verbs ("was made," "to give") are just mechanical placeholders for the exciting (or troubling) content of the sentence—which is found in the nouns. Notice how the sentence can be improved by replacing the dodo verbs with the hidden ones:

> We decided not to subsidize students.

In general, you should seek verbs that are vivid, active, or part of a process that can be seen, imagined, or felt:

> When I <u>find</u> a job on the employment board, I <u>feel</u> exhilarated.

> I <u>haunted</u> the mail box for half a year, <u>waiting</u> for a response from the Social Security Administration.

> <u>Commit</u> yourself to becoming a better writer.

> <u>Creating</u> comedy routines gives me great pleasure.

> In a courtroom lawyers often <u>say</u> whatever outrageous comment comes to mind.

> Inflation <u>results</u> directly from high employment.

Not all "dodo verbs" need replacement. For example, it would be difficult to write on any subject for a length of time without using the verb "to be." We are simply advising you to pay attention to a few of these verbs in proofreading, and make replacements when they seem to improve the sentences.

EXERCISE 11-2

Circle the dodo verbs in the following sentences. Replace those or recast the sentences where improvement seems possible. Place an "A" by those where the verb seems appropriate.

1. This problem of spelling is one of the most troublesome that make up my writing.

2. A rat does a lot of things when it is confronted with various stimuli.

3. When poverty-stricken adolescents have help, they make better citizens.

4. The president had imagined nettlesome difficulties in the coming elections.

5. Most work is boring.

6. Do not pass GO. Do not collect $200.

7. Difficult questions on exams make me think.

8. Policemen do many things when they stop a car on the freeway.

CLICHÉS

Choosing words carefully and effectively requires pruning clichés from your writing and replacing them with more vivid, more accurate word choices. What is a cliché? Some of your former instructors may have labeled it a "hackneyed" or "trite" expression. It is an overused expression that has lost its power to inform or intrigue a reader. The word cliché comes from the French *clicher* which means to make a metal printing plate from a casting—obviously such a process suggests language and ideas that will be used over and over ad nauseam. Imagine that on your typewriter, instead of having only keys for letters of the alphabet, you had keys with the following expressions.

SOME CLICHÉS IN COMMON USE

dead as a doornail
from the bottom of their
    hearts
like a needle in a haystack
as the saying goes
so to speak
the bottom line
to be brutally frank
a far cry
conspicuous by its absence
supreme moment
in the final analysis
sharp as a tack
it goes without saying
last but not least
from the frying pan into
    the fire
to make a long story short
that is neither here nor
    there
light as a feather
kill two birds with one
    stone
for the birds
make the most of it
a blessing in disguise
it was like a bad dream
others only dream about

hard-earned cash
not as easy as it sounds
get on the ball
a sight for sore eyes
always there when I needed
    him/her
a job well done
making me the person I am
    today
make or break
where you are coming from
take the good with the bad
works hard all his life
go hand in hand
all walks of life
get my act together
in the same boat
in today's world
red as a rose
as slow as molasses in
    January
an idea whose time has
    come
she's her own person
throughout all history
pure as the driven snow
I love her dearly
everyday you can see
    something new

Such a typewriter might seem to save you a lot of time, but of course most readers would just slide over such expressions, having seen them so many times before. Clichés are clichés because they are so popular—they have caught on and become widespread. So do not be particularly surprised or embarrassed if you catch yourself employing them—almost everyone does. What you want to do as a proficient writer is to recognize that you have written a cliché, then omit or revise it.

Of course one of the reasons a cliché becomes popular is that once upon a time (another cliché?) it was fresh, vibrant, and innovative. Someone thought it up, spoke it, wrote it down, and impressed her friends. They were so impressed that they began to use the expression, and it spread like wildfire (another cliché). And so, very soon, the expression was no longer impressive—not new, vibrant, or imaginative. In fact, no reader or writer would even *think* about what it meant. For example, once someone[1] compared a virgin to the whiteness of snow—"she was pure as the driven snow"—especially when it is blown about before it hits the ground. And for those familiar with snow, this seemed a particularly evocative combination of the ideas of naturalness, whiteness, and purity. Finally the cliché became so overused that hardly anyone used it anymore—perhaps it even sounds old-fashioned, to you— this is the fate and danger of many clichés. Tallulah Bankhead (1902—1965), a stage actress and screen star not particularly noted for her sexual circumspection, once made this cliché come alive by inverting it, claiming she was "pure as the driven slush." Notice how that phrase leads the reader into a reawakening and makes him reexamine the idea, the image, the speaker, nature, and notions of purity. Thus inversion may be one way of using a cliché effectively. You will probably have noticed that many of the clichés listed you have never used, and perhaps some are based on concepts we no longer understand (What is a "doornail"? Why is it so dead?).

EXERCISE 11-3

In the following selections, identify the cliches and either omit them entirely or find fresher alternatives as substitutes.

1. As a breed, the college administrator is as slow as molasses in January.

---

[1]The literary sources go back to Shakespeare's *Hamlet* (III,i,142), but the ultimate origin is probably from a significantly older folk source.

2. Being forced to take anthropology was a blessing in disguise. Though I was stubborn as a bulldog at first, eventually I came to be intrigued by the diversity of cultures different from my own.

3. The director of the childcare center sticks in my mind. She was her own person—took ballet on the side, went mountain climbing in the summer, and still had an intrinsic understanding of child psychology that exceeded that of any textbook.

4. If the Federal Reserve Board were to lower the discount rate, it would not only affect member banks' prime rates, but would affect people from all walks of life.

5. To be brutally frank, I hated English throughout my entire life, from the first grade up to the college proficiency exam—and even after.

6. In the final analysis, most human relationships these days suffer from too much communication, rather than a failure to communicate.

7. To make a long story short, in conclusion I decided to transfer from electrical engineering to psychology because I found exploring human personality more fascinating than designing abstract patterns on silicon chips.

8. Trying to find a lyric poem celebrating the joys of accountancy was like trying to find a needle in a haystack.

9. It goes without saying that a quarterback must be quick, intelligent, and have steady hands.

10. Jacob could discern immediately where I was coming from when I began to ask him where he took his degree in psychology.

REDUCING WORDINESS

You need to pay attention, especially while proofing, to wordiness. Wordiness is the tendency to overwrite or use more words than needed to express an idea. Just as certain vague, bland words and dodo verbs lend a sloppy, colloquial effect to your writing, a regular pattern of unnecessary words can annoy a reader, slow down your discussion, and, in effect, leave you less to say. You might think of wordiness as a problem of efficiency—the proficient writer learns to use words skillfully so that none are wasted; the proficient writer uses a minimum number of words to get a message across. Wordiness occurs when many more words are used than needed to express an idea:

Many of these experiences occur during the many hours when I use my car to travel along the roads from one place to another in order to get somewhere.

New innovations are constantly being created by our creative, technologically oriented, society.

It seemed that I was feeling a hatred for the woman who was my mother, whose name was Jane, a hatred so intense that it resulted in bitter feelings.

At this point in time, the doctor had begun the initiation of a process that would lead to removal of the patient's gall bladder.

Each and every student must take into account the problems attendant on becoming a student.

Each of these sentences can be made leaner through careful pruning, the process of carefully cutting away words that don't add meaning or emphasis so that your ideas actually become clearer and more emphatic—just as in gardening, you prune away excess foliage so that the plant grows more quickly or into an attractive shape. This "word pruning" will save the reader time and make your sentences more emphatic. It will also allow you time to devote effort (and perhaps add sentences or paragraphs) to other portions of your essay—where such effort will increase proficiency. Here are suggested revisions:

These experiences occur primarily when I travel by car.

Our technologically oriented society constantly produces innovation.

My hatred for my mother, Jane, was so intense it produced lasting bitterness.

Then the doctor operated to remove the gall bladder.

Each student encounters serious problems.

There are many methods you can use to prune unnecessary words. But remember, any method is an art, not a science—and that, particularly under the time pressure of exam conditions, you need not feel compelled to produce a flawless paper, without a single unnecessary word. If you know that wordiness is one of your writing problems, you should practice to reduce it in all your writing. Proficient writers often revise their drafts numerous times—and they sometimes find unnecessary words even on the final reading. We suggest you try to employ some of the following methods to reduce wordiness:

- Avoid essayese.

- Question whether "I think," "I feel," "it seems" and other hedges add any useful information to your sentence.

- Avoid "there is," "there are," "who is," "which is," "that is," "it is," "it was."

- Seek the hidden verb.

- Reduce repetitive phrases to a single word.

- Replace roundabout expressions with concise alternatives.

Avoid Essayese

Many students state explicitly that their essay, or a paragraph, "intends to do such and such." Often they use this **essayese** to pad their writing, and fill an essay with many references to what they are doing or will do in a sentence or a paragraph. This practice is not only wordy—it is annoying; it reminds a reader that he is reading words on a page rather than engaging ideas or participating vicariously in experiences. Readers generally don't like to be reminded they are readers, any more than movie patrons like it when the film stops in the middle, or the lights go on, or there is some interruption that reminds them they are participating in an illusion. Here are some typical examples of essayese:

> I want to discuss what I consider the most important event in my life, the birth of my son, and describe the experience.

> This essay will examine the problem of nuclear power, then I will consider alternatives to nuclear power, then I

will offer a solution, and finally I will conclude by summing up what I have learned.

In conclusion, I have told a story about my addiction to cocaine and crank, explained how I solved the problem that I have, and suggested strategies to cope with the problem.

As I have previously stated in my first paragraph, the social welfare system in this country costs too much and achieves too little.

I am going to write about the contradictions in feminism as I see them.

Instead of telling the reader what you are going to write, just write it. Avoid essayese by carefully re-examining the introduction and conclusion (where it usually occurs) and focusing intently on sentences with words such as the following: *write, essay, paragraph discussion, conclusion, conclude, stated.* Revise by omitting or recasting those sentences:

My son's birth affected my life more than any other event.

Nuclear power is but one of many fuel alternatives: by considering other sources, we can solve the problems of nuclear power.

So in 1985 I became addicted to cocaine and crank because of my emotional needs, but I have recently found strategies to avoid using these dangerous drugs.

To reiterate: the social welfare system in this country costs too much and achieves too little.

Feminism exhibits a number of contradictions.

Avoid Unnecessary Hedges

Overuse of "I think," "I believe," "I feel," "it seems," and "it is my opinion that" usually indicates that the writer is unsure and wishes to hedge in some way, in order to avoid criticism. Ironically, phrases like these DO NOT emphasize or strengthen opinions, nor do they protect writers from readers who disagree with the opinions. Most readers won't find your writing any more persuasive because you constantly reiterate that the information provided is not factual and may be questioned. Furthermore, readers understand that the sentences and words on the paper are *your* perceptions, thoughts, and feelings because *you* wrote them. Readers understand that any *good* essay is based on informed opinion and is not merely a collection of facts. So to write "I think" or "I feel" is to tell the reader what he or she already knows. Perhaps once or twice in a 700-word essay you can intensify or personalize a thought by adding these phrases, but it is generally more effective to avoid them. Consider the following writing examples:

> I think that higher education spends too much time on requirements and too little on individuals.

> I feel that the drug problem in our nation needs serious attention.

> It seems that the computer has as many advantages as disadvantages.

Revising these types of wordiness is easy: omit the unnecessary words. The remaining words will usually stand alone as a sentence:

> Higher education spends too much time on requirements and too little on individuals.

> The drug problem in our nation needs serious attention.

> The computer has as many advantages as disadvantages.

Remove Placeholder Words

Many of us write sentences which begin "There is" (or "There are," "It is") or that contain relative clauses introduced by "which is" (or "who is" or "that is"). Often these phrases simply contain **placeholder words** or function words that help make a sentence complete but offer no information to the reader. Pruning such words can be an effective way to achieve more powerful sentences—sentences that are leaner, clearer, and have more words devoted to content. Consider the following examples of sentences made wordy by placeholder words:

> There is a problem of homelessness confronting our nation.

There are many general education classes I have taken.

The Vietnam War, which was the longest war in our history, resulted in over 50,000 deaths of American soldiers.

Albert Einstein, who is the greatest scientist of the twentieth century, was also politically active and was enlisted by numerous social causes.

It is important to write clearly and avoid wordiness.

Removing the placeholder words is often the quickest solution to this problem; sometimes the sentence needs to be slightly restructured—simply look for another verb:

A problem of homelessness confronts our nation.

I have taken many general education classes.

The Vietnam War, the longest in our history, resulted in over 50,000 deaths of American soldiers.

Albert Einstein, the greatest scientist of the twentieth century, was also politically active and was enlisted by numerous social causes.

Writing clearly and avoiding wordiness are important.

Seek The Hidden Verb (See also the earlier section on dodo verbs.)

In the first sentence of the last group of examples, we reduced wordiness by replacing the verb "is" with the verb "confronts." We call this process **seeking the hidden verb.** You might have noticed that "confronts" was in the original sentence as "confronting." Many times you can make your sentences more proficient by finding a verb hidden in a noun or adjective, then recasting the sentence to make that hidden verb the *main verb* (sometimes you may have to find a new subject, or identify a subject that had been previously only implied). For example here are several common expressions that can easily be made more proficient by seeking the hidden verb and recasting the phrase:

WORDY	PROFICIENT
We will make the determination	We will determine
It is our understanding that	We understand that
He will make use of	He will use

Usually the hidden verb is more specific, more visual, or indicates action more than the original verb in the sentence. The following sentences are wordy partially because a more effective verb is hidden (the hidden verb is <u>underlined</u>):

Our refusal was the <u>cause</u> of his disappointment.

You must have a <u>plan</u> so that your <u>performance</u> has the proper result.

The <u>specifications</u> in the rules are that <u>information</u> can be given only to department chairs.

In all these examples, the hidden verbs are actually *nouns:* the cause, a plan, your performance, the specifications, that information. Note how making the hidden verbs function as actual *verbs* improves these sentences:

Our refusal caused his disappointment.

You must plan so that you perform well.

The rules specify that you should inform only department chairs.

Reduce Repetitive Combinations To Single Words

Sometimes unwary writers form phrases in which one word unnecessarily repeats the idea of another:[2]

new innovation—An innovation is a new idea or invention.

true facts—Facts are called facts because they are true.

each and every—Both "each" and "every" single out objects one at a time and include the universe. (In general, a tendency to pair adjectives or verbs with "and" should be occasionally investigated to see that you are not repeating or offering a meaningless additional distinction.)

reflect back—When you reflect, you think *back*.

---

[2]Some writers prefer to call this wordiness problem "redundancy."

Note how the following sentences use these repetitive combinations:

> Edison's light bulb was a new innovation.
>
> One of a police officer's prime duties is to ascertain the true facts.
>
> Each and every student must register and pay fees in advance.
>
> When I reflect back on my childhood, I encounter only a series of disappointments.

We hope you can see that eliminating one of the repetitive words **does not** change meaning and improves the sentence as well:

> Edison's light bulb was an innovation.
>
> One of a police officer's prime duties is to ascertain the facts.
>
> Every student must register and pay fees in advance.
>
> When I reflect on my childhood, I encounter only a series of disappointments.

Here is a list of other repetitive combinations to avoid or prune:

final outcome	red in color
advance planning	small in size
basic fundamentals	past history
dead corpses	advance warning
initial onset	joined together
surrounded on all sides	

Replace Roundabout Expression With Concise Alternatives

Many of us get into the habit of writing long-winded, roundabout expressions when simpler, clearer, shorter alternatives are available. Often we do this simply because we have seen others use the expression, because it is common in a place of business or in the culture at large, or because we have the mistaken notion that the longer version is more impressive, more serious, more awe-inspiring. Consider the following alternatives to roundabout expressions:

Roundabout Expression	Concise Alternative
at this point in time	then
at the present time	now
along the lines of	similar
because of the fact that	because (*or* since)
for the reason that	because (*or* since)
in the near future	soon
in very few cases	seldom
with reference to	about
is of the opinion that	thinks (*or* believes)
in accordance with	by
in the nature of	like
in the event that	if
in the majority of instances	usually, frequently, often
a small number of	few
there have been times	sometimes

Roundabout expressions make many sentences tedious and difficult to read, even though they often give the impression of expertise, intelligence, or careful precision. Though they seem to add importance or sophistication to an idea, they don't. You should learn to avoid them.

EXERCISE 11-4

Prune wordiness from the following selections by using some of the techniques we have suggested (such as avoiding essayese, seeking the hidden verb).

1. In the following essay I will try to explain how I came to choose my career path at this point in time. First, I will describe my experience in high school. Then I will analyze how I view the job market. Finally, I will conclude by showing that my career choice of electrical engineering was a natural one.
2. At the present time there is no new innovation on the horizon in the automotive industry.
3. I think that a serious problem confronting our country at this point in time seems to be the issue of people who are abusing drugs.

4. Each and every consumer must try to discover his or her own way to reduce the cost of groceries by comparative shopping and coupon clipping.
5. The reason that English is the dominant language in our country is because of the fact that the earliest settlers with significant global political power were from England.
6. Hemingway reflected back on his early life in the city of Paris in writing his famous book called *A Moveable Feast*.
7. It was necessary for the perfecters of the personal computer to first break down their problem into separate tasks; then it was important for them to assign each and every task to a separate individual engineer.
8. I am of the opinion that in the near future the human immune system will break down completely and totally, and the cold virus will be in the position to rule the world.
9. In very few cases there is someone who stands above his fellows and is able to pierce right to the very core of any and all problems which he might be faced with in his life.
10. Because of its refusal to find an answer to the questions which were put by the lawyer, the jury was unable to determine a conclusion to its deliberations.

We have saved for last this chapter on choosing and pruning words because some of you will not need it and because the information in the other chapters is usually far more critical to improving your writing. If you focus first on the Rules of Thumb (see Chapter 2), you will generally improve your writing so that you will pass a proficiency exam. Still, many of you may find helpful the hints we offer here, and these hints may lead you to a general interest in the improvement of your writing, so that you will not simply pass a proficiency exam, but will excel and earn a distinctive score.

SUMMARY

1. In revising for word choice you need only make a few, subtle changes to improve the clarity and power of your writing.
2. Change bland, general words such as "thing," "people," and "interesting" to more specific words.
3. Be concrete—reduce your use of abstract or general words.

4. Replace some "dodo" verbs ("is," "make," "do") with "hidden verbs."
5. Learn to recognize clichés, and replace or omit them as you are writing (or revising).
6. Reduce wordiness by avoiding essayese, hedges, and "there is" constructions. Seek verbs hidden in nouns and adjectives. Reduce repetitive phrases to a single word. Replace roundabout constructions with concise alternatives.

AFTERWORD:

NOW THAT YOU HAVE PASSED A PROFICIENCY EXAM

We hope and assume that you will have passed your proficiency exam by the time you reach this chapter. At this point some of you may be tempted to "be done with" what you have learned in this text or from the course that might accompany it.

However, we believe that the skills suggested here have far broader application than merely passing a proficiency exam. Though in this text we have focused primarily on the writing strategies for a proficient essay, we would like to remind you how you can use these in the future and how you might consider additional strategies for writing in the "real world."

First, try to remember that Proficiency Exams, artificial as they may seem, are considered by states and educational institutions to be the most efficient and fairest method of measuring key or crucial skills in all students. Still, exam designers and English professors know (as you do) that most of us write better when given more time and when we are allowed to write about what we know or about material we have chosen. Other advantages of the non-test situation include being able to use a word processor, being able to collaborate on writing with peers, and being able to use a habitual process for discovering writing material.

Most of your writing from now on will probably conform to these conditions. Nevertheless, whether you are instantaneously given a question by a proficiency exam tester, assigned a writing task by your supervisor at work, or begin to write on your own about something that interests you, it will help you to follow many of the Rules of Thumb from Chapter 2.

You will still need a time/task plan. Undoubtedly your time available will be expanded, but it will not be infinite. A plan will help you to separate the tasks involved in your writing problem into discrete stages and elements and to assign a provisional time block to each one. It will also help if you start writing immediately by brainstorming a series of suggestions or random thoughts and committing these to paper.

One benefit of not being in a two-hour test situation is that you can take advantage of "incubation." After initial planning and brainstorming (and perhaps at several later stages in composition), you can afford to take a break. You may wish to let your subconscious mind deal with the writing task in an unfocused way overnight, for a few hours while you pay attention to another task, or in some other way.

You also should strive, early in your writing process, to focus your ideas into a thesis (or hypothesis—a temporary structure you may later abandon or modify). Try to write in one sentence a road map of where your writing will go.

As you write, try to keep paragraphs developed and focused by avoiding one-sentence paragraphs and one-page paragraphs. At some point try to bring your writing to a close with a concluding section. Be careful, especially in long-term projects, to leave time for proofreading. However, once you are not bound by exam rules, you may find it helpful to enlist a friend or colleague in mutual proofreading. Proofreading aloud also becomes a far more practical strategy when you are not in an exam room. Some of you may find most of your spelling problems (but not doubles) solved by running your composition through a word processor's "spellcheck" program.

Not all writing consists of exam questions, assignments, or supervisors' queries. Some of you may discover that you really enjoy writing and are challenged by it. Rather than waiting for an external demand, you may find that keeping a journal of your thoughts or responses to daily stimuli may provoke you to writing in a far more creative way.

We expect that most of you will be surprised by how often you will write seriously in the future. We hope this text has given you the confidence in your abilities to write proficiently, and has helped you to see writing as a powerful skill that can be enjoyed and employed, rather than an onerous school-task to be endured or avoided.

APPENDIX A

ANSWER KEY TO SELECTED EXERCISES

(Corrections are underlined or circled.)

CHAPTER 8

8-1

1. Fragment: In just a minute⊝ I'm going to lose patience with this task.
3. Comma splice: Gunner is a college senior⊙ his sister runs a beauty shop.
5. Comma splice: Our employee incentive plan is simplicity itself⊙ make one mistake and you're fired.
7. Correct.
9. Run-on sentence: Kim worked all night⊙ that's why she's sleeping now.
11. Correct.

8-2

(Changes are indicated for the first two paragraphs only.)

One professor I had was particularly annoying⊙ especially because of his habit of giving unannounced quizzes on difficult homework⊝ for example⊙ five pop quizzes in one month. He would assign, say, 60 pages of reading in modern physics⊙ then the next class day he would give us a 20 question quiz on the difficult parts of the homework, such as ⊝equations for the theory of relativity or Schrodinger's wave equations.

But he was not the only professor with a distinctive behavior that interfered with my learning⊝not at all. A history professor expected us to memorize the dates of every significant event in the last hundred years⊝even events I considered insignificant⊝and I stayed up all night trying to memorize those dates. We had to memorize dates such as the following⊙ when World War I began; when it ended; when the two atomic bombs were dropped on Japan; when the Watergate break-in occurred; and many other seemingly obscure dates. And⊙ needless to say⊙ I failed.

8-3

(**Note:** Underlining shows corrections, not subjects or verbs.)
1. Correct.
3. My reality and my education <u>are</u> very important to me.
5. There is <u>a difference</u> of opinion among authorities who are involved in the study of criminal behavior.

7. The ceiling, as well as the walls, <u>is</u> freshly painted.
9. Correct.
11. Correct.

8-4

1. No one wanted <u>her</u> picture taken. (*Or:* No one wanted <u>a</u> picture taken.)
3. The company moved <u>its</u> office to San Francisco.
5. <u>Each girl</u> must pay her <u>deposit</u> before leaving on her trip.
7. Both the Joneses and Mr. Smith enjoyed <u>their</u> trip.
9. Nobody understood where <u>he</u> went wrong on the quiz.

(**Note:** There is no reason to specify either gender in #1 or #9.)

8-5

1. A student⊙s first duty is to his or her education.
3. The man-of-war⊙s naval architecture was effective in its time, but a distinct disability in the following age.
5. Correct.
7. The Ellerbees⊙ home was a raucous place—full of dirty diapers, unpaid bills, broken furniture, and an undiminished sense of humor.

8-6

1. By the time Willa Cather became editor of *McClure's Magazine* in New York, she <u>had lived</u> in Virginia, Nebraska, and Pennsylvania. She <u>had been</u> strongly influenced by her years in Pittsburgh.
3. I get lonely when I am tired, when I <u>spend</u> too much time with strangers, or when my emotions <u>get churned</u> up.

8-7

1. It⊙s not always important whether you're rich or not.
3. When the grades came out, it was a great pleasure for <u>me</u> to see the A beside my name.
5. <u>Their</u> problem was that they could not understand <u>whether</u> to perform the experiment first or apply for the funds first.
7. I was fixing the car myself, but I <u>knew</u> that I would have to call the mechanic in two hours and pay an outrageous bill.
9. The <u>effect</u> of that symphony on <u>me</u> was greater than I knew.

CHAPTER 9

9-1

1. main subject = <u>penny saved</u>
   main verb = <u>is</u>

2. main subject = <u>swimming</u>
   main verb = <u>is</u>
3. main subject = <u>Tom</u>
   main verb = <u>asked</u>
4. main subject = <u>mansion</u>
   main verb = <u>stood</u>
5. main subject = <u>computer</u>
   main verb = <u>refused</u>
6. main subject = <u>map</u>
   main verb = <u>is</u>
7. main subject = implied <u>you</u>
   main verb = <u>say</u>

(**Note:** Example #7 is a sentence in which the subject is *implied,* or *understood.* This type of sentence is called an **imperative sentence,** or a **command sentence,** and it is the only instance in which the subject may be omitted but implied. The single word "Elizabeth!" is called an **interjection**— a single-word exclamation that adds intensity to the message in the sentence that follows it.)

9-2

1. Fragments: <u>yelling at the kids to get ready on time</u>
   <u>barely made it to school on time</u>
   Suggested correct version: It was a frustrating morning. <u>I was yelling at the</u>
   <u>kids to get ready on time.</u> Then we rushed out the door <u>and barely made</u>
   <u>it to school on time.</u>
2. Fragments: <u>in buckets</u>
   <u>flooded the streets, the gutters, the driveways</u>
   Suggested correct version: It didn't just rain; it poured <u>in buckets.</u> It
   <u>flooded the streets, the gutters, and the driveways.</u> We thought it would
   never stop.
3. Fragment: <u>although I hate getting up early</u>
   Suggested correct versions: I'm taking an 8:00 a.m. class this semester
   <u>although I hate getting up early.</u> The discipline is good for me. *(or)* I'm
   taking an 8:00 a.m. class this semester. <u>Although I hate getting up early,</u>
   the discipline is good for me.
4. Fragments: <u>whereas others enjoy living in the city</u>
   <u>despite all the traffic</u>
   Suggested correct version: Some people enjoy living in remote spots
   <u>whereas others enjoy living in the city, despite all the traffic.</u>
5. Fragments: <u>whenever I look at Vicky</u>
   <u>as if I have known her in a past life</u>

Suggested correct version: <u>Whenever I look at Vicky, I get a strange feeling.</u> <u>It is as if I have known her in a past life.</u>

9-3

1. dependent words = whenever
                                             which

dependent clauses = <u>whenever I feel depressed</u>
                                        <u>which always cheers me up</u>

2. dependent words = even though
                                             because
                                             who

dependent clauses = <u>even though the chocolate mousse tasted like chalk</u>
                                        <u>because she didn't want to disappoint the chef</u>
                                        <u>who had worked so hard to prepare it</u>

3. dependent words = as if
                                             that
                                             once

dependent clauses = <u>as if having the leading part in the play were a great</u>
                                            <u>hardship to her</u>
                                        <u>that she would never act again</u>
                                        <u>once the play was over</u>

4. dependent words = whereas
                                             since

dependent clauses = <u>whereas my sister Fran has listened to nothing but</u>
                                            <u>the Beatles</u>
                                        <u>since she was five years old</u>

9-4

1.
a. independent clause
b. dependent clause
c. phrase
d. dependent clause
e. phrase
f. dependent clause
g. independent clause
h. phrase

2.
a. dependent clause
b. dependent clause
c. phrase
d. dependent clause
e. sentence
f. phrase
g. sentence
h. dependent clause

Students should write their own sentences using the phrases or dependent clauses in #a, b, c, d, f, and h.

9-5

Following is a revised version of the paragraph with comma splice and fused sentence errors corrected. Correct punctuation is circled.

As an artist, Mary Cassatt was unique in several ways. First, she was a woman; most women of her time did not aspire to careers in the arts. In fact, it was so unusual for a woman to succeed in the arts that many female writers of the time, such as the Brontes, wrote under male pen names just to get their work published. Cassatt did not let her gender stop her from developing her talent as an artist. She was, in fact, the only really important female artist and the only significant American painter to become an expatriate in France. She was also the only American to be accepted into the central French Impressionist group. Another aspect of Cassatt's life that was different than most artists of her time was that she came from a wealthy family. Her father was a wealthy banker. She and her family lived elegantly in Paris or in the French countryside as she pursued her career as an artist and later an art collector. She had no financial worries.

CHAPTER 10

10-1

1. Marge had the class with Joanne Jencks, who was a part-time instructor. (C3)
3. Correct.
5. Because I was unable to understand the simplest concepts of algebra, I failed math in high school three times. (C2)
7. My first stop is always at the popcorn counter, and my last stop is always at the men's room when I go the movies. (C1)
9. Males — and females alike find politics fascinating as a spectator sport. (No comma necessary)
11. Thin, rich, really attractive women used to be popular in cigarette ads. (C4)

10-2

1. Before you can expect to pass an exam, you must study.
3. The man looked silly in his very old, worn-out, blue—plaid shirt.
5. Michael visited the following places: Dallas; Rome; New York; Boise, Idaho; Los Angeles; and Seattle, Washington.
7. We bought the following items at K-Mart: new boots, a watch, a vacuum and towels.
9. Correct.
11. Susan likes living in Maine—even though the winters are very cold.

10-3

(We have suggested a possible punctuation scheme for the first three sentences. While it is clear that punctuation is necessary, several other alternatives would also be effective. The purpose of the exercise is to help you see how different pieces of punctuation interact to give the reader helpful cues.)

California is conventionally divided in half⊖into Northern California and Southern California⊖the division occurring just North of the Tehachapi Mountains. The two are very different⊙ they are almost like two separate states. Northern California is⊖to select a few details⊖San Francisco⊙ Santa Cruz⊙ Yosemite⊙ the Redwood forests, the white-water rafting rivers⊙ the state Capitol⊙ environmentalists⊙ and assorted crazies.

Chapter 11

(The first three exercises have so many possible alternatives, equally good, that a key would be misleading. Here are a few suggestions for how to prune the verbiage from exercise 11-4.)

11-4

1. My career choice—electrical engineering—stemmed naturally from my experience in high school and my current analysis of the job market.
3. Drug abuse is a serious issue that confronts us.
5. The English language dominates in our country because the earliest settlers with political power were from England.
7. The perfecters of the personal computer first had to break down their problem into separate tasks; then they assigned each task to a separate engineer.
9. Very seldom does anyone stand out from the mass as a universal problem solver.

APPENDIX B

CORRECTION SYMBOLS

ANT   Faulty antecedent or ambiguous antecedent for a pronoun

AGR   Faulty agreement: singular subjects take singular verbs; plural subjects take plural verbs. Singular pronouns should have singular antecedents; plural pronouns should have plural antecedents.

AMB   Ambiguous construction

AP   Faulty use of apostrophe; or, apostrophe needed here to show possession.

AWK   Awkward construction—revise this sentence; put your hand over it and try saying aloud what you think it means.

CAP   Capitalize the first letter of this word.

CE   Comma error: No comma is needed here [if a comma is present]; or comma is needed here [if none present]

CH   Choice: This word seems poorly chosen—consult your dictionary or thesaurus; see if you can find a more precise, exact, or specific word.

CL   Clarity: This sentence or paragraph is unclear; perhaps you need another sentence to clarify your use of these particular words.

COL   Colloquial: inappropriate level for this assignment or context—too much like casual speech

CONC   Conclusion

CS   Comma splice: It is confusing to use a comma here to join these two independent clauses—use a semicolon or period.

D   Diction: This word is not appropriate for the occasion; it is too formal or informal; it doesn't fit the context of sentence or paragraph.

DOUB   Wrong choice from a pair of "doubles"; use the other word (other spelling)—for example, "too" for "to."

DM   Dangling modifier: This word, phrase or clause is improperly placed in the sentence; its grammar suggests that it modifies the subject, but this is not the case here.

FRAG Sentence fragment: This fragment lacks a subject or a verb and is therefore not a sentence—often it can be corrected by a punctuation link to the previous sentence.

FS Fused sentence: These are two independent clauses requiring clarifying punctuation (semicolon or period) to separate them.

GEN Too general, vague or abstract; be more specific—aim for an event that occurred one time at one place.

H Hackneyed: trite; a cliché; avoid expressions such as these that lack freshness, seem tired, mechanical, or overused.

ID Faulty idiom: Usually you have chosen the wrong preposition for the particular verb—test by seeing how this expression sounds out loud.

INT Introduction

LOG Faulty logic—unconvincing

MM Misplaced modifier: This word belongs elsewhere in the sentence—follow the arrow to the proper place.

MIX Mixed construction: This sentence began with one grammatical pattern (for example, subject, verb, object), then without warning changed to another pattern mid-sentence. There are parts of two sentences here—the best correction is to turn each into a complete sentence.

OBV Obvious: overgeneralization. This is true all the time, everywhere and for virtually every reader; therefore it is a waste of ink and time—omit.

P Error in punctuation

REF Pronoun reference: A pronoun is used here to refer to a noun, but the noun doesn't exist or is unclear. Often the pronoun is used to stand for all of a sentence or paragraph. Make the reference more specific by referring to an idea (for example, "this *problem*").

REP Repetitious: You've said this already, too much the same way, or too many times.

RED Redundant: You've used two different words that mean nearly the same thing, so your sentence is actually repetitious.

ROS	Run-on sentence: Same as FS
SE	Semicolon error: You've used a semicolon incorrectly, or you need a semicolon here.
SP	Spelling error
T	Tense of verb here is inappropriate: It is inconsistent with other tenses used in the sentence, paragraph, or essay.
TRANS	Transition fault: There is no transition or only a weak transition; link the idea in this paragraph to the paragraph before, so it is clear how the two are related.
V	Verb form error: Check verb conjugation in a dictionary.
W	Wordiness: Too many words used in the sentence to make the point you want to make. You're wasting your time on this—go on to a new topic.
WW	Wrong word: The word used here doesn't fit the context—check a dictionary for meaning.
¶	Paragraph: Begin new paragraph here.
NO ¶	No paragraph: The material in this paragraph should be connected to the one before.
‖	Faulty parallelism: Items in series are not the same mode or number or part of speech.
?	What do you mean here? I don't understand; this sentence doesn't make sense.
[ ]	Omit: Take out these words or sentences—they are unnecessary.
∧	Some necessary words have been omitted; put them in.
✔	Important point; needs to be made; I'm glad to see you put it in.
GOOD	Better than the check mark above: I'm impressed; this is really original thinking.